THE WAY
PEOPLE
LIVE

Life on a
New World Voyage

THE WAY PEOPLE LIVE

Life on a
New World
Voyage

Titles in The Way People Live series include:

Cowboys in the Old West
Games of Ancient Rome
Life Aboard a Space Station
Life Aboard the Space Shuttle
Life Among the Aztecs
Life Among the Great Plains Indians
Life Among the Ibo Women of Nigeria
Life Among the Inca
Life Among the Indian Fighters
Life Among the Pirates
Life Among the Puritans
Life Among the Samurai
Life During the American Revolution
Life During the Black Death
Life During the Crusades
Life During the Dust Bowl
Life During the French Revolution
Life During the Gold Rush
Life During the Great Depression
Life During the Middle Ages
Life During the Renaissance
Life During the Roaring Twenties
Life During the Russian Revolution
Life During the Spanish Inquisition
Life in a California Mission
Life in a Japanese American Internment
    Camp
Life in a Medieval Castle
Life in a Medieval Monastery
Life in a Medieval Village
Life in America During the 1960s
Life in an Amish Community
Life in a Nazi Concentration Camp
Life in Ancient Athens
Life in Ancient China
Life in Ancient Egypt
Life in Ancient Greece
Life in Ancient Rome
Life in a Wild West Show

Life in Berlin
Life in Castro's Cuba
Life in Charles Dickens's England
Life in Communist Russia
Life in Genghis Khan's Mongolia
Life in Hong Kong
Life in Moscow
Life in the Amazon Rain Forest
Life in the American Colonies
Life in the Australian Outback
Life in the Elizabethan Theater
Life in the Hitler Youth
Life in the Negro Baseball Leagues
Life in the North During the Civil War
Life in the Stone Age
Life in the Warsaw Ghetto
Life in Tokyo
Life in War-Torn Bosnia
Life of a Medieval Knight
Life of a Nazi Soldier
Life of a Roman Gladiator
Life of a Roman Slave
Life of a Roman Soldier
Life of a Slave on a Southern Plantation
Life on Alcatraz
Life on a Medieval Pilgrimage
Life on an African Slave Ship
Life on an Everest Expedition
Life on a New World Voyage
Life on an Indian Reservation
Life on Ellis Island
Life on the American Frontier
Life on the Oregon Trail
Life on the Pony Express
Life on the Underground Railroad
Life Under the Jim Crow Laws
Life Under the Taliban

THE WAY PEOPLE LIVE

Life on a New World Voyage

by Andrew A. Kling

LUCENT BOOKS

An imprint of Thomson Gale, a part of The Thomson Corporation

THOMSON
™
GALE

Detroit • New York • San Francisco • San Diego • New Haven, Conn. • Waterville, Maine • London • Munich

LIBRARY OF CONGRESS CATALOGING-IN-PUBLICATION DATA

Kling, Andrew A., 1961–
    Life on a new world voyage / By Andrew A. Kling.
        p. cm. — (The way people live)
    Includes bibliographical references and index.
    ISBN 1-59018-163-8 (hardcover : alk. paper)
    1. America—Discovery and exploration—Juvenile literature. 2. Transatlantic voyages—History—Juvenile literature. 3. Immigrants—America—History—Juvenile literature. 4. America—Emigration and immigration—History—Juvenile literature. I. Title. II. Series.
    E121.K55 2004
    970.01—dc22
                                                                                        2004010850

Printed in the United States of America

Contents

Discovering the Humanity in Us All

Books in The Way People Live series focus on groups of people in a wide variety of circumstances, settings, and time periods. Some books focus on different cultural groups, others, on people in a particular historical time period, while others cover people involved in a specific event. Each book emphasizes the daily routines, personal and historical struggles, and achievements of people from all walks of life.

To really understand any culture, it is necessary to strip the mind of the common notions we hold about groups of people. These stereotypes are the archenemies of learning. It does not even matter whether the stereotypes are positive or negative; they are confining and tight. Removing them is a challenge that is not easily met, as anyone who has ever tried it will admit. Ideas that do not fit into the templates we create are unwelcome visitors—ones we would prefer remain quietly in a corner or forgotten room.

The cowboy of the Old West is a good example of such confining roles. The cowboy was courageous, yet soft-spoken. His time (it is always a he, in our template) was spent alternatively saving a rancher's daughter from certain death on a runaway stagecoach, or shooting it out with rustlers. At times, of course, he was likely to get a little crazy in town after a trail drive, but for the most part, he was the epitome of inner strength. It is disconcerting to find out that the cowboy is human, even a bit childish. Can it really be true that cowboys would line up to help the cook on the trail drive grind coffee, just hoping he would give them a little stick of peppermint candy that came with the coffee shipment? The idea of tough cowboys vying with one another to help "Coosie" (as they called their cooks) for a bit of candy seems silly and out of place.

So is the vision of Eskimos playing video games and watching MTV, living in prefab housing in the Arctic. It just does not fit with what "Eskimo" means. We are far more comfortable with snow igloos and whale blubber, harpoons and kayaks.

Although the cultures dealt with in Lucent's The Way People Live series are often historically and socially well known, the emphasis is on the personal aspects of life. Groups of people, while unquestionably affected by their politics and their governmental structures, are more than those institutions. How do people in a particular time and place educate their children? What do they eat? And how do they build their houses? What kinds of work do they do? What kinds of games do they enjoy? The answers to these questions bring these cultures to life. People's lives are revealed in the particulars and only by knowing the particulars can we understand these cultures' will to survive and their moments of weakness and greatness.

This is not to say that understanding politics does not help to understand a culture. There is no question that the Warsaw ghetto, for example, was a culture that was brought about by the politics and social ideas of Adolf

Hitler and the Third Reich. But the Jews who were crowded together in the ghetto cannot be understood by the Reich's politics. Their life was a day-to-day battle for existence, and the creativity and methods they used to prolong their lives is a vital story of human perseverance that would be denied by focusing only on the institutions of Hitler's Germany. Knowing that children as young as five or six outwitted Nazi guards on a daily basis, that Jewish policemen helped the Germans control the ghetto, that children attended secret schools in the ghetto and even earned diplomas—these are the things that reveal the fabric of life, that can inspire, intrigue, and amaze.

Books in The Way People Live series allow both the casual reader and the student to see humans as victims, heroes, and onlookers. And although humans act in ways that can fill us with feelings of sorrow and revulsion, it is important to remember that "hero," "predator," and "victim" are dangerous terms. Heaping undue pity or praise on people reduces them to objects, and strips them of their humanity.

Seeing the Jews of Warsaw only as victims is to deny their humanity. Seeing them only as they appear in surviving photos, staring at the camera with infinite sadness, is limiting, both to them and to those who want to understand them. To an object of pity, the only appropriate response becomes "Those poor creatures!" and that reduces both the quality of their struggle and the depth of their despair. No one is served by such two-dimensional views of people and their cultures.

With this in mind, The Way People Live series strives to flesh out the traditional, two-dimensional views of people in various cultures and historical circumstances. Using a wide variety of primary quotations—the words not only of the politicians and government leaders, but of the real people whose lives are being examined—each book in the series attempts to show an honest and complete picture of a culture removed from our own by time or space.

By examining cultures in this way, the reader will notice not only the glaring differences from his or her own culture, but also will be struck by the similarities. For indeed, people share common needs—warmth, good company, stability, and affirmation from others. Ultimately, seeing how people really live, or have lived, can only enrich our understanding of ourselves.

A New World for Europeans

Christopher Columbus's arrival in the New World, although an accident, was an event that changed the world. Columbus had intended to reach the riches of Japan, India, and China by sailing west from Spain across the Atlantic Ocean, instead of attempting the difficult voyage around Africa.

Though Columbus was correct in suggesting that the world was round, he was not the first to do so. In fact, the idea had first been proposed by the ancient Greeks. Nor was he the first European to reach the New World; recent archaeological evidence reinforces Scandinavian oral histories that recount voyages to what is today Canada almost five hundred years before Columbus.

In 1492 Christopher Columbus and his crew make landfall in the New World.

Three ships full of colonists arrive at Jamestown, Virginia, in 1607. By the end of the seventeenth century, more than a million Europeans had come to the New World.

However, Columbus and many others underestimated the size of the planet, and this miscalculation became painfully obvious as he and his small flotilla made their way across the Atlantic in 1492. Consequently, this voyage took longer than Columbus had estimated. More important, he made landfall not in China, Japan, or India, but in what was truly, to European eyes, a new world.

Although Columbus died firmly convinced that he had reached the mystical lands of the East, voyages made by other mariners, explorers, and adventurers soon made it clear that there was a great land mass between Europe and the East. These new lands were collectively called the New World, in contrast with the "old world" of Europe and the Middle East. And with each new adventurous and difficult voyage across the Atlantic Ocean, the knowledge of the New World grew. Sailors talked about the natives and their customs; explorers wrote about the different plants and animals; and mapmakers attempted to create an accurate picture of lands that were new to Europeans. With each ship that returned from the New World, people's curiosity grew, and each successive voyage brought more and more Europeans to the shores of the New World.

However, there were those who exaggerated the conditions of these new lands. The early Spanish explorers wrote glowing reports of the abundance of precious metals. One early English explorer described his time in a newly explored land as if he had "bene in the midst of some delicate garden abounding with all kinds of odoriferous flowers."[1] The first European colonists often found conditions much more difficult than they had been led to believe. Yet many sent positive reports of their colony back to Europe with the ships returning from the New World.

More and more Europeans followed the first voyagers across the Atlantic Ocean. From the days of Columbus to the close of the seventeenth century, more than a million Europeans crossed the Atlantic Ocean. The New World, and the brave colonists who arrived there, would never be the same.

Ships and Crews

In the sixteenth and seventeenth centuries, daring European explorers made countless voyages across the Atlantic Ocean. Each ship that returned brought stories about new lands and new people across the seas. Soon, everyone wanted to learn about these lands of North, Central, and South America, then called the New World. And across Europe, there was no shortage of individuals—sailors, ships' captains, and even monarchs—willing to risk an investment of time or money in a journey to the New World.

The Promise of Great Rewards

Each person involved in such a venture expected great rewards. The monarch who sponsored the voyage hoped to become king or queen over newly discovered lands; one

A fanciful woodcut depicts King Ferdinand of Spain observing Columbus's arrival in the New World.

English mariner John Davis was an outspoken supporter of English voyages to the New World. In his 1594 book *The Seamans Secrets*, he expressed the opinion that England, through the leadership of Queen Elizabeth I, could become a wealthy nation:

"For what hath made the Spaniard to be so great a Monarch, the commander of both Indies, to abound in wealth & all natures benefits but only the painful industry of his subjects in Navigation, their former trade was only figs, oringes, and oyl, but now through Navigation is brought to be gold, silver, pearls, silks, and spice, by long and painful trade recovered. Which great benefits only by her Majesties loving clemency and merciful favour he doth possisse: for if her Highnesse and her most honorable Lords would not regard the small distance between her Dominions and those fameous rich Kingdoms, the easinesse of the passage being once discovered (the North west I mean) with the full sufficiency of her Highnesse subjects to effect the fame, there could then be no doubt, but her stately seat of London should be the store house of Europe, and nurse to all Nations, in yielding all Indian commodities in a far better condition, as a more easie rate than now brought unto us exchanging commodities of our own store, with a plentiful return at the first hand, which now by many exchanges are brought to us."

English king instructed an adventurer to "seek out, discover and finde whatsoever isles, countrey regions or provinces"[2] previously unknown to Europeans. The captain wished to find a new river or bay that led inland to the rumored cities of gold. Perhaps he might even find what fabled mariner Christopher Columbus had not: a direct route to the fabulous wealth of what was then called the Indies. These lands—India, Cipango (now Japan), and Cathay (now China)—were the sources of prized luxuries in Europe, such as silk and spices. And the crew hoped that if they were not the first to discover a route to the Indies, they would at least be able to reach the New World and share in some of its great wealth of gold and silver.

Each of these potential rewards came with risks. For the ruler, commissioning, outfitting, and sponsoring a voyage was a time-consuming and expensive venture involving little personal danger. But there were tremendous personal hazards involved for the captains and the crews. An ocean voyage was always a dangerous undertaking, a venture from which there might be no return. Consequently, many mariners followed the known route pioneered by Columbus.

Temporary Rest Stops

Columbus's chosen route west across the Atlantic Ocean minimized the dangers of the North Atlantic Ocean. In the days of sailing vessels, and particularly in the early days of transoceanic voyages, it was difficult for a ship to make way against a headwind, which blows from the direction the ship is heading. Ship and sail design limited the mariners' ability to make progress against such a prevailing wind. For example, if a captain wished to sail south, and was confronted with a southerly headwind, he had two choices. He could try to sail "close to the wind," sailing as close to due south as possible by carving a zigzag pattern, east and then west, but moving a little bit south on each leg. This tedious practice, called tacking, keeps the ship in motion but often results in little direct progress toward the ship's destination. The other choice was to find a safe port or take down his sails and wait for the wind to change direction.

Columbus understood that he would be confounded by westerly headwinds in the North Atlantic. But he knew the wind patterns were different off the coast of Africa, so he attempted a route that, according to historian Samuel Eliot Morison, was based on his many years of sailing experience:

He . . . would run south before the northerlies [i.e., sail south with the winds behind him] prevailing off Spain and North Africa to the Canary Islands and there make, as it were, a right-angle turn. For he had observed on his African voyages that winter winds in the latitude of the Canaries blew from the east.[3]

Columbus's route was followed by successive Spanish explorers in their voyages to the New World. The Canary Islands, off the west coast of Africa, or the Azores Islands, due west of Portugal, offered the last opportunity for hundreds of miles for westbound mariners to stock up on essential supplies, including freshwater and live animals for food.

Past the Canaries and the Azores, there was only empty ocean awaiting ships, captains, and crews heading west. In order to make a safe and successful crossing, ships usually traveled in groups. This minimized the risks to the expedition, as additional ships could help if one or more companion ships encountered difficulties during the voyage. Additionally, every man aboard needed to know his responsibilities and had to perform them skillfully. (These sailing vessels had no female crew members. In the minds of these mariners, women were too weak to withstand the hard work involved in an ocean voyage, and were considered bad luck aboard a ship.) And at the head of each of

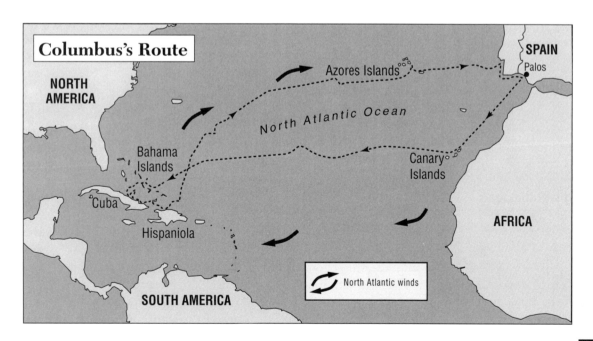

Columbus's Route

these voyages, responsible for understanding and delegating all of those duties, was the ship's captain.

The Role of the Captain

In this age of exploration, it was common for a captain to offer his services to anyone who would pay him. Consequently, an English ship might be commanded by a French or Italian captain. The explorer born Giovanni Caboto in Venice, Italy, took the English name John Cabot when he sailed under the English crown. As commander, the captain was responsible for all actions of his crew, for safeguarding the well-being of the crew, and for ensuring that the voyage was as successful as possible.

That success depended on the captain's skills as a mariner. The best captains were skilled at determining the direction of the wind, the direction of the prevailing current, and the progress of their ship. Additionally, they were keen observers of the weather, understanding that a shift in the wind might forecast a coming storm. Yet even the most astute captain was sometimes caught by an ocean storm. In the face of such dangerous circumstances, a ship's captain relied on the expertise and experience of his crew members. One of these specialists was the navigator, called the pilot.

The Pilot

In the days of the first journeys across the Atlantic Ocean, the pilot was perhaps the most important person aboard ship after the captain. His skills in navigating the ship and determining its location at any time were essential.

However, even skilled mariners knew very little about their position on earth. They could not measure longitude (position east or west) with any certainty; indeed, instruments to accurately measure this did not exist until the late 1700s. For the sixteenth- and seventeenth-century navigator, any measurement of longitude as his ship sailed across the Atlantic was merely a guess.

The pilot determined his longitude through a process called dead reckoning. This was an estimate of the ship's position given its speed and direction. He used the ship's sand-glass (similar to an hourglass) and a device called a log line to measure how far the ship traveled in a given span of time. He combined this figure with the bearing read from the ship's compass to estimate the distance and speed traveled.

In contrast, the ship's latitude (its position north or south of the equator) could be measured with reasonable accuracy. To determine latitude, these early pilots used an instrument called a cross-staff.

Latitude, the Sun, and the Stars

The pilot used the cross-staff to observe either the sun or the North Star. The cross-staff allowed him to determine the star's altitude above the horizon, which was a close approximation of the ship's latitude.

Ideally, these readings were taken at exactly noon, but it was not uncommon for the sun to be obscured by clouds at that time. The navigator also took readings at dawn as the sun rose above the horizon, measuring the angle between it and the North Star. Once he had made his computations and established the ship's position, he consulted with the captain, who determined if the ship should stay on its current course or if a new course was

The role of ship captain carried a great deal of responsibility. The captain was accountable for the actions and well-being of the entire crew, and the success of the voyage was dependent on his skills as a mariner.

Calculating Ship's Speed

Calculating the ship's speed was essential for the pilot to determine the ship's location through dead reckoning. Author Peter Whitlock, writing for the Web site *The Mary Rose*, described a method for calculating ship's speed using a log line:

"The log was used to measure the speed of a ship through the water. A piece of wood with a 'stray' line attached was thrown off the stern of the ship until it floated clear. This stray line was in turn attached to a rope reeled on a hand held drum. As the ship moved away from the floating log the reel turned and the rope was allowed to run off for a specified period of time measured by a sand glass. The line was marked by knots in the rope at proportionate distances and at the end of the specified period the number of knots to run off the reel was recorded. . . . The log and sand glass combination gave the speed of the ship, with the course being obtained from the compass. This information was plotted on the 'traverse board,' a form of peg board on a compass rose. Pegs were inserted every half hour of a four hour watch to show course and estimated distance covered. This information would be interpreted by the pilot and [he] could now estimate his east-west distance traveled to give him longitude."

necessary. This information was then passed on to the helmsman.

At the Helm

Then as now, the helmsman steered the ship. He made sure the ship changed course when necessary and stayed on that route for as long as ordered. In the age of sailing vessels, this was difficult, as ocean currents and wind direction often pushed ships off course. The helmsman's main job, therefore, was to ensure that the chosen route was followed as closely as possible.

For example, if the captain selected a course due west, a wind coming from the southeast could push the ship to the north of its intended course. The helmsman therefore had to keep an eye on his compass and sandglass to ensure that the ship was pointed just south of west. This helped him keep the ship moving consistently to the west.

These minor variations were easily accomplished in good weather, but if the wind and the waves became forceful, the helmsman became less concerned with course than he was with survival. A storm might lead the captain to order a new course, and the helmsman needed to turn the ship without mishap; if turned the wrong way in high winds and rough seas, the vessel could be damaged by waves smashing its hull, or it could overturn.

After the storm passed, the captain, the pilot, and the helmsman tried to determine the ship's location and the best way to return to their original course. Often the men simply headed for the nearest land, especially if the ship needed repairs.

The Carpenter

Ships that traveled to the New World in the sixteenth and seventeenth centuries were built of wood. And each ship, no matter how expertly built, required the attention of the ship's carpenter during the voyage. He was responsible for checking the condition of each wooden part of the ship, from the smallest part of the system of masts, booms, and spars, called rigging, to the hull of the ship itself, making repairs whenever necessary. According to Morison, the carpenter and his assistant "performed all the necessary repairs to the wooden fabric and spars, and saw to it that topsides and decks were properly caulked and the seams payed [filled] with pitch."[4]

Each ship's hull was made of hundreds of individual pieces, and the gaps where pieces met were filled with rope soaked in a type of tar called pitch. Maintaining the caulking and the pitch in each seam of the ship was of utmost importance. Any seam might leak during a voyage, even when the ship was not in motion.

As the ship sailed, the carpenter and his mate studied the seams, determined which seams required more attention than others, and worked to ensure that minor leaks did not become major ones. The carpenter consulted with the ship's officers, who sometimes assigned members of the crew to assist with repairs or to man the pumps deep in the hull of the ship.

Prince Henry (aka Henry the Navigator) calls for a new voyage of exploration. Ocean currents and wind direction often pushed ships off course, and it was up to the captain and helmsman to follow their designated route as closely as possible.

Using a Cross-Staff

A cross-staff was an instrument used for obtaining latitude at sea. At the Meridian, or 12 o'clock noon, the pilot measured the angle between the sun and the area directly overhead, called the zenith. Holding the cross-staff at eye level and adjusting the crosspiece, called a transversary, enabled him to obtain his general latitude. English mariner John Davis, in his book *The Seamans Secrets*, describes how to find latitude at sea using a cross-staff:

"Place the Cross-Staff to your Eye, . . . then move the Transversary upon your Staff to and fro as occasion requireth, until at one and the same instant you may set by the upper edge of your Transversary, halfe the body of the Sun, or Stars, or that the lower edge of or end thereof so likewise touch the Horizon, at that place where it seemeth that the skie and the Seas are joyned, having special regard in this your observation, as that you hold the Transversary as directly uprightly as possible you may, and you must begin this observation somewhat before the Sun or Stars be at South, and continue the same so long as you perceive that they rise: for when they are at the biggest, then are they upon the Meridian, . . . at which time they will be due South from you if your Compass be good and without variation, and then both the Transversary shew upon the staff the degrees and minutes that the said body is from your Zenith . . . unto that number so known by your instrument . . . is the Poles height, or the Latitude of the place where you are."

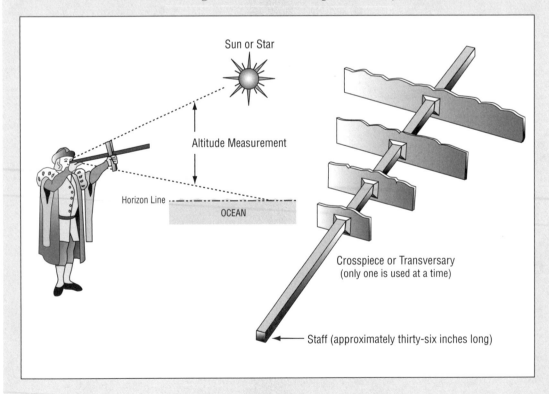

Sun or Star

Altitude Measurement

Horizon Line

OCEAN

Crosspiece or Transversary
(only one is used at a time)

Staff (approximately thirty-six inches long)

This illustration depicts fifteenth-century carpenters at work on the hull of a ship. The hull was built with hundreds of individual wood pieces.

The carpenter's job was sometimes dirty and grueling, and he often worked out of the sight of the men, but his accomplishments were usually immediately apparent to officers and the crew. A leak that was quickly slowed or stopped, or a piece of rigging that was artfully repaired, meant that he had done his job well. The men were thankful to have a competent carpenter on board.

Food and Drink for the Officers and Crew

There was one member of the crew who was not as well received by his shipmates. The cook had perhaps the most thankless job on a voyage to the New World in the sixteenth and seventeenth centuries. Although the welfare of the entire crew depended on his abilities, the cook rarely received compliments if the crew was well fed and happy. However, he was quickly the target of scorn if the food supplies spoiled or ran out.

The cook was responsible for buying supplies before departure, replenishing items at stops such as the Azores or the Canaries, and preparing each meal of the voyage. But the combination of limited storage space and the primitive knowledge of proper nutrition meant that the sailor's diet was quite monotonous.

Although occasionally the men might catch some fish during the voyage, most of their food was brought on board at the start of their journey. According to historian David Beers Quinn, "the basic food supply [included] salt[ed] cod and . . . dried cod, ling, and conger eel, meat in barrels, followed by beef and pork, beans and peas, and some vinegar."[5] However, the most common food for sailors of this day was a concoction of flour and water called hardtack.

Hardtack and Other Victuals

Hardtack, a type of dry biscuit that was baked on shore before departure, was the staple food for the men on the early New World voyages. It was the main item at each meal, day after day, week after week. Sometimes it was the only food available. The cook tried to keep it as dry as possible, but invariably the wooden casks in which it was stored became damp and the hardtack began to rot. Columbus's son Ferdinand recalled that on one of his father's voyages, "I saw many who waited for darkness to eat the porridge made of [hardtack], that they might not see the maggots; and others were so used to eating them that they didn't even trouble to pick them out because they might lose their supper had they been so nice."[6]

The crew had little choice but to eat the spoiled hardtack. Their daily rations were limited by the ship's storage capacity and they needed to get as much energy as they could from what they were issued. According to author Daniel Francis, when English explorer Martin Frobisher departed England to explore what is now Canada in the 1570s, his crew's daily rations were fairly meager: "Fro-

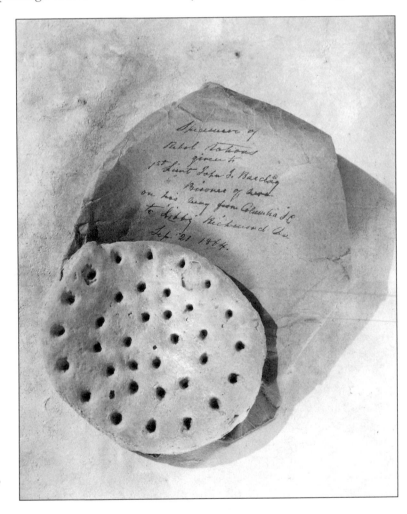

Pictured is a preserved hardtack biscuit from the Civil War. Hardtack was a staple food for crews on New World voyages.

bisher's men . . . received daily a half-kilogram of dry biscuit, four liters of beer (preferable to water, which went stale), a kilogram of salt meat, some dried peas, a quarter of a salted fish, and some butter, cheese, rice, oatmeal, raisins and nuts."[7]

The ship's officers fared somewhat better. The cook usually provided other victuals (foodstuffs) for them at the start of the voyage, such as fresh fruit and vegetables and fresh meat, before he turned to salted pork or fish.

Feeding upward of three dozen men and officers occupied most of the cook's waking hours. He spent the rest of his time taking stock of the supplies and trying to keep them from spoiling or being eaten by rats and insects.

Keeping the Ship Shipshape

The rest of the crew aboard an early voyage to the New World consisted of young men and boys. They were responsible for all the other functions associated with a sailing vessel, and were often a mix of experienced sailors and young boys, sometimes only eight or nine years old, who were new to the sea. Except for the youngest boys, each could perform virtually all the tasks required to keep the ship shipshape, or in good working order. Most of these tasks were associated with the sails.

Sails were the main means of propulsion for these ships. Wind filled the sails and pushed the ship forward. Sails were raised, lowered, and furled, or rolled up to reduce their size, using ropes called lines. The sails were pulled into position by brute strength. They were tied up, or lashed, into the rigging that towered above the ship's top deck, and were removed only in emergencies, such as a storm. Each time a sail needed to be furled or

unfurled, men scrambled into the rigging, wrestled the sails into place, and lashed them into position. When a sail needed to be repositioned to take advantage of a wind shift, or to change course, men on deck grabbed the lines attached to the corners of the sail to haul it into place. It was an arduous task when winds were light or moderate, and downright dangerous when storms arrived.

Sails were made of cloth, and cloth wears out. The men maintained the sails by sewing or repairing seams and patching worn spots with other bits of cloth. The lines also wore out with use. On a daily basis, the crew repaired frayed lines by splicing their ends together. Occasionally, they had to climb out onto a spar to cut loose a stray end of a line so that it could be spliced into a new rope. Lines were recycled whenever possible.

Housekeeping on a New World Voyage

Unlike lines and sails, which were repeatedly repaired and recycled, many items on board these ships were simply thrown overboard when they were no longer useful. Animal bones, broken drinking cups and utensils, and other objects that could not be repaired or used for some other purpose were tossed into the sea. Human waste was disposed of through a makeshift toilet—a hole in the floor of a deck that sat out over the water.

However, some items were too valuable to discard, no matter what their condition. Crewmen ate out of wooden bowls, while officers usually used bowls and platters made of pewter. After each meal, the utensils and bowls were rinsed with seawater, as freshwater was far too precious to be used for washing. These tasks were part of a daily routine that varied little from day to day once a group of ships put to sea.

Establishing and Enforcing the Rules

Before a ship left port, the captain addressed his crew, announcing what he wanted the voyage to accomplish and what he expected of them. He warned that members of the crew who did not meet his expectations or who violated his code of conduct would be punished. Threats of physical violence, such as whipping, with the number of lashes increasing with each offense, were seen as a deterrent to wrongful behavior. Men might be lashed for falling asleep on duty, failing to perform an assigned task, or questioning an order. Additionally, as the crew was often a mix of men from different backgrounds, men were lashed for getting into fights over ethnic or racial comments. They could even be punished if an officer only suspected them of disobedience.

European mariners of the time understood the treatment they faced if they violated the rules. In fact, one sixteenth-century account of shipboard punishment claimed that ships' boys were punished on such a regular basis "that some meere seamen and saylers doe believe in good earnest that they shall never have a faire winde until the poor boyes be duly . . . whipped every Mondaye morninge."[8]

With the code of conduct firmly established, the ship's officers assigned men to a daily routine that kept the essential functions of the ship manned twenty-four hours a day. This was, and is still today, called the watch system.

Watches

Every watch was under the command of a particular officer. The captain, the pilot, the ship's master (the captain's second in command) and the master's mate (the captain's third in command) each commanded a watch. Each day had six watches of four hours each, generally changing at 4, 8, and 12 o'clock, day and night.

Columbus addresses his crew at the start of their voyage. The ship captain typically established a code of conduct for his crew that included harsh corporal punishment for violators.

Each watch had a boy whose sole job was to watch the sandglass. This enabled the crew to keep an accurate gauge on the passage of time. When the sand passed from the top to the bottom of the glass, thirty minutes had passed, and the boy called out that the glass was being turned. Each watch was four hours, giving eight turns to a watch.

The seventh turning of the glass was important to the next group of men slated to be on watch. The report of the turning of the glass at 7:30 A.M. was a warning to the next watch to get ready to come on duty. The watch coming on duty at 8:00 A.M. had some break-

fast (usually featuring the ubiquitous hardtack), scrubbed down the deck, and manned the pumps deep in the hold, or the lowest part of the ship, to remove whatever water had leaked in through the hull overnight.

The men worked hard during their watch. Hauling lines by hand, repairing lines and sails, and keeping the ship shipshape was rigorous work, even in pleasant weather. Consequently, men rested as much as possible when they were not on duty. Those men going off watch at 8:00 A.M. also had breakfast and most sought a place to sleep out of the sun, either belowdecks or on deck in the shade. There

One of the types of vessels used for New World exploration was a sailing ship called a caravel. It was large enough to carry crew and cargo across the Atlantic Ocean, yet small enough to sail in and out of shallow coastal waters. Author Diane Sansevere-Dreher, in her book *Explorers Who Got Lost*, describes the ship's advantages:

"The design of the caravel produced speed and maneuverability. Unlike the big, round-bottomed carracks, which were made for holding large cargoes, the caravel had a slimmer hull and a shallower keel. These features gave the caravel greater speed and allowed it to sail into shallow harbors and inlets. Another important feature was the fact that it was "lateen-rigged," with big triangular sails. The triangular sail could be set on either side of the mast to take advantage of the wind. Most caravels had two masts, each with its own lateen sail. Later caravels added a third mast that carried a square-rigged sail. This provided a wider surface of canvas to take advantage of stiff ocean winds. In contrast, carracks were "square-rigged," with rectangular sails set at right angles to the mast. These sails worked well when the wind blew from behind, but they were not good when the wind was blowing from the side, or when the ship had to sail into the wind."

was no privacy on board these early ships, and no bunks for the men; they usually slept in a corner where they could prop themselves against the rolling of the ship.

Aside from sleeping and eating, there was little for the men to do but to stay out of the way of the men on duty. For entertainment, they often told tall tales, called sea yarns. The longer the vessel was at sea, the longer the opportunity existed to create and embellish the tales. The best stories kept the men entertained throughout their time off watch until it was time to go back to work.

However, there were times when every man was called to duty, regardless of which watch he was on. The watch officer's cry of "All hands!" rousted everyone on board to the top deck, ready for anything.

"All Hands!"

The command for "All hands!" usually meant that the ship faced an emergency, such as a powerful storm. In such an emergency, each second could mean the difference between survival and death. Orders from the captain and his officers had to be carried out swiftly. Watches were abandoned during these situations, although the sandglass was still turned and the boys still marked the time.

Once the emergency had ended, the captain and crew had to deal with the aftermath. The routine of watches needed to be reestablished as soon as was practical, but this might take a day or more. Many men might be needed to pump a ship or to make repairs, such as fashioning new sails from ones ripped apart by a storm or improvising rigging to replace spars and yardarms carried away by the heavy winds and seas.

No doubt during the long and arduous hours and days during and following an emergency, some of the crew may have doubted the outcome of their voyage. According to English adventurer Richard Hawkins, some captains in one such storm-tossed fleet wished to return to England as quickly as possible:

One [captain], with a little blustering wind taketh occasion to loose company [leave the other ships]; another complaineth that he wanted victuals; another, that his ship is leak[ing]; another, that his mastes, sayles, or [lines] fayleth him.[9]

Hawkins felt that, among this fleet, "the willing never want [for] probable reasons to further their pretences"[10]—in other words, that the other captains and crew were making up excuses to discontinue the venture. Perhaps these men thought that no matter what discoveries they might make in the New World, no reward was worth the danger.

Discoveries and Rewards

By the middle of the seventeenth century, it had become apparent that the natives of North America had no vast treasure troves of

Caravels were designed for speed, but they were large enough to carry sizable crews and cargo. Pictured are Columbus's three caravels: the Niña, Pinta, and Santa Maria.

After returning from a voyage to Newfoundland, John Cabot petitions King Henry VII of England to sponsor a second voyage to the New World.

gold, silver, and other minerals. This was a huge disappointment to many who had made the voyage, who faced another arduous crossing of the Atlantic before they could gain any reward for their efforts.

Many captains were rewarded upon their return to Europe with property, money, or ships to make additional voyages. For example, when John Cabot returned to Bristol, England, in 1497 after making landfall at what is today Newfoundland, King Henry VII granted Cabot permission to make another voyage, providing more ships and more money.

Yet for many of the crewmen who had sailed to the New World and back, there were no rewards. None of them made a personal fortune from the voyages. The vast majority were illiterate and their impressions were not included in the official accounts of the voyages. In these accounts, the hardships of the voyage were minimized, if they were mentioned at all. Morison writes that "we can imagine [Cabot's crew] telling unbelievable fish stories in Bristol, and grumbling about the fog, the chill and the mosquitoes"[11] as well as the gales that they had encountered during the journey. Despite the crew's complaints, Henry VII and other monarchs continued to sanction voyages.

The glowing official reports of these voyages began to have an effect on the people of Europe. The officers, captains, and financiers boasted of a New World across the sea that was waiting to be explored and exploited for its natural resources. A new generation of men soon emerged willing to risk their lives and fortunes—and their families—in a bid not only to cross the Atlantic, but to stay there. They became the first European colonists in the New World.

Preparing to Emigrate

In 1587 the English scientist Thomas Harriot composed a small book that was widely read throughout Europe. Written in the flowing style of the day, *A Briefe and True Report of the Newe Found Lands of Virginia* is today considered an unparalleled eyewitness account of coastal North Carolina and Virginia. However, Harriot's intention in publishing this book was not simply to describe the parts of North America he had visited. One of his main goals was to interest other Englishmen in colonizing the New World. His book and others like it were instrumental in helping to spread the word about the New World. They helped many individuals to decide to take the monumental step of signing up for a voyage to the New World.

Taking the First Step Takes Money

Many of the first European settlers were gentlemen. These young men—from England, Spain, France, Sweden, and the Netherlands—came from a variety of backgrounds. Some were distantly related to the ruling royal families. Some were sons of wealthy landowners or of prosperous merchants. Despite their differences, however, all these gentlemen had at least two elements in common: They had decided that their fate lay across the Atlantic in the New World, and they had enough money to afford to join a proposed colonizing effort.

In the early days of European efforts to colonize the New World, each colonist spent his own money to outfit himself with the necessary equipment for his new life and to purchase necessary supplies for the voyage and for the colony's early days. He was also expected to commit a portion of his personal fortune to help outfit the ship; this money assisted the colonial organizers who were doing the planning but would not make the actual voyage.

A Variety of Expenses

The expenses associated with preparing to join a colonizing effort were considerable. Historian David Beers Quinn wrote that looking back on the early days of English colonial efforts, "it is impossible to find out what the minimum subscription was for a man, or for a family, but it cannot have been too small."[12] At this time in England, a quart of beer cost a halfpence, and a lodger could stay at a tavern, with meals included, for six pence a day. The total cost of the suggested items amounted to a considerable expense at a time when a gentleman's yearly income might be less than five hundred pounds a year. One of the early voyagers to Massachusetts, John Josselyn, listed dozens of items that each family would need to bring with them for a new life in the New World, from common items such as nails, axes, and hatchets, to items such as a "canoe [costing] 3 pounds" and a "chain and lock for a boat [costing] 2 shillings two pence."[13]

In addition, in 1600s England, the typical fare for a passenger over five years old was £5. The fare alone was equivalent to approximately £360, or $640, today. Therefore, colonial organizers tried to recruit individuals who had money to spare.

The first Europeans to create permanent colonies in the New World were the Spanish. They established settlements on the islands of the Caribbean Sea and on the mainland of Central and South America.

The Spanish System

The men who joined Spain's early colonies were largely motivated by financial interests, as they hoped to make their fortune in the New World. Thousands of young men wished to make the voyage across the Atlantic, but the Spanish government was reluctant to allow unregulated emigration. It wanted to ensure that only certain segments of the population joined the Spanish colonies. According to historian Marilyn C. Baseler,

Spain . . . chose to conserve its domestic population by regulating Spanish emigration. Licensing procedures . . . [meant that] the cost of obtaining the documents necessary for emigration prevented impoverished Spaniards from using the New World as a place of new beginnings.[14]

These restrictive policies meant that between 1492 and 1700, only about 3,750 Spaniards left Europe for the New World each year. The Spanish colonists were followed by English, French, Dutch, and Swedish gentlemen who also ventured across the Atlantic to their nations' New World colonies.

A Gentleman's Motivation

In sixteenth- and seventeenth-century Europe, the oldest son in a family—particularly a wealthy one—inherited the lion's share of his father's possessions, particularly when it came to the father's landholdings. Only when landholdings were very large could the estate be divided among all the sons.

Arthur Barlowe in the New World, 1584

In an attempt to interest their fellow Englishmen in the portion of North America that would eventually be called Virginia, Arthur Barlowe wrote in glowing terms about an area he felt was a paradise on earth. His account of his 1584 voyage to what is now the Outer Banks of North Carolina, quoted in David Beers Quinn's *Set Fair for Roanoke*, includes this vivid description:

"We viewed the land about us, being whereas we first landed, very sandy but low towards the water side, but so full of grapes as the very beating and surge of the sea overflowed them, of which we found such plenty, as well here as in all places else, both on the sand and on the green soil on the hills, as in the plains, as well as on every little shrub, as also climbing towards the tops of the tall cedars, that I think in all the world the like abundance is not to be found: and myself, having seen those parts of Europe that most abound, find such difference as were incredible to be written."

The Spanish were the first Europeans to establish permanent colonies in the New World. Here, the island of San Salvador is claimed for Spain.

In many cases, such as in England, where estates were smaller and there were fewer opportunities to purchase undeveloped land, younger sons realized that they might not be able to own land. Those who had money to spare left home in search of new opportunities, and the prospect of creating new life in the New World was a strong motivation for many of these gentlemen.

The Problem with Gentlemen

The Spanish colonial organizers were the first to discover that gentlemen did not make the best colonists. These first settlers had been drawn to the idea of colonization much as mariners of the day had been; they expected to make their fortunes in these new lands with little or no effort. Many were ill-suited for the hard work that awaited in the New World.

Developing and maintaining a colony was harder work than expected. The colonists not only had to plant and tend to crops, they also had to build and maintain structures for housing and storage. Even Christopher Columbus, one of Spain's most ardent promoters of colonization of the New World, had to admit that he and his men were underprepared. He sent trusted associates back to Spain with letters for his king and queen, begging for more supplies:

These provisions should continue until we have obtained the produce from all we have seeded and planted, by which I mean wheat, barley and vines. . . . We also need live sheep—preferably male and female lambs—several small calves and a few small heifers sent to us whenever any ship comes our way.[15]

Other European nations, particularly England and France, encountered similar problems during their early colonial efforts. Author François Bellec wrote that these gentlemen experienced a harsh New World reality:

The . . . gentlemen . . . discovered the hard labor of a farming colonist in a country where nothing existed. This existence was quite different from the promised gold deposits, which were supposed to be so abundant that they were to gather the precious ore by the handful.[16]

Colonists use shovels and pickaxes to dig the foundation for Saint Augustine,
Florida, the first permanent European settlement in the United States.

These experiences led to a shift in the methods used to recruit future colonists.

Other Recruits

The New World captivated the attention of more than just the wealthy few in Europe. Tales of the experiences of explorers and colonists came back across the Atlantic and became available in publications such as Harriot's *A Briefe and True Report* and Richard Hakluyt's *Voyages to the New World.* These were widely read and discussed throughout Europe. The lessons learned by the early colonial ventures led organizers to look beyond their nation's wealthy citizens.

Organizers of the English colonies began to recruit members of England's middle class, those who had made a successful living as merchants and traders, did not have the benefit of family fortune, and were more accustomed to hard work than gentlemen were. Quinn, describing one of England's sixteenth-century colonial ventures, wrote that the organizers concentrated on the capital city of London. Based on the surviving written evidence, he surmised:

> These people intended to sell their property, or borrow on the strength of it, and they were not coming to America without adequate equipment or assurance of money behind them to finance future supplies when they arrived. Thus the venture can be thought of as . . . a mainly middle-class group which was not satisfied for some reason with its prospects at home, and, at the same time, was enticed by the prospects abroad.[17]

Organizers found that these individuals were more willing than gentlemen to leave England for the New World. After all, a gentleman still had the prospect of inheriting an estate or the family fortune if his older brother or brothers died; a middle-class merchant did not.

Deciding to Leave

It cannot have been an easy decision to leave one's home for a new and unfamiliar land. For some people, positive news from the New World made the decision an easier one. Richard Saltonstall, who had voyaged to the new English colony in Massachusetts in 1631, wrote to a friend in London, "Therefoer good Sir incourage men to come over for heare is land & meanes of lively hood sufficient for men that bring bodys able, & minds fitted to brave the first brunts, which the beginings of such workes necessarily put men upon."[18]

Another Englishman, Roger Clap, noted in a memoir that when he became apprenticed to a Mr. Mossiour, he began to hear of New England for the first time and of the

> many godly persons that were going there. . . . My master asked me whether I would go? I told him, were I not engaged unto him I would willingly go; he answered me that should be no hindrance. . . . I then wrote to my father . . . to intreat his leave to go to New-England; he was so much displeased at first, that he wrote me no answer, but told my brethren that I should not go.[19]

His father eventually relented, and the twenty-year-old Clap emigrated in 1630.

For others considering emigration, the health of their family was an important matter. If a man's wife was pregnant, he had her health and the health of the baby to consider.

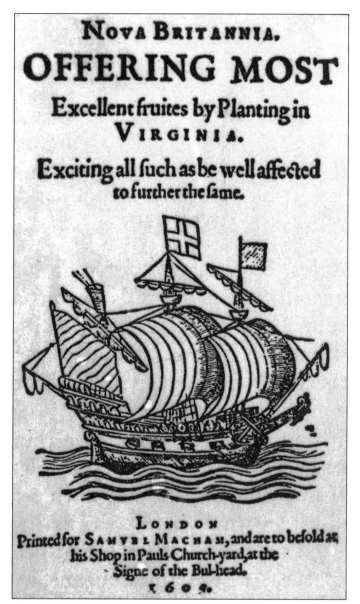

The London Company printed this pamphlet in 1609, promising great rewards to industrious colonists in Virginia.

Even so, there were several circumstances that might lead them to opt for their departure despite the pregnancy. For example, a child expected in August might delay the journey by a year if the family had to wait until another passage was available once baby and mother were healthy enough to make the trip. The family might not be able to afford a passage if they waited another year. These kinds of factors had to be taken into consideration.

Religious Considerations

Many people emigrated to escape religious persecution by the rulers and citizens of their

Royal Proclamation from King Charles I

On April 30, 1637, England's King Charles I issued "A Proclamation Against the Disorderly Transporting His Majesties Subjects to the Plantations Within the Parts of America," which expressed his concern over the large-scale immigration of English to the New World. The proclamation appeared in "British Royal Proclamations Relating to America, 1603–1783," in volume 12 (1911) of the American Antiquarian Society's *Transactions and Collections.*

"The Kings most Excellent Majestie being informed that great numbers of His Subjects have bin, and are every year, transported into those parts of America, . . . and there settle them selves, some of them with their families and whole estates amongst which numbers there are also many idle and refractory humors, whose onely or principall end is to live as much as they can without the reach of authority: His Majestie having taken the premisses into consideration, is minded to restraine for the time to come such promiscuous and disorderly departing out of the Realme; And doth therefore straitly charge and command all and every the Officers and Ministers of his severall Ports. . . . That they doe not hereafter permit or suffer any persons . . . to embarque themselves in any of the said Ports, or the members thereof, for any of the said Plantations, without Licence from His Majesties Commissioners for Plantations first had and obtained in that behalfe; Nor that they admit to be embarqued any persons . . . without an Attestation or Certificate from two Justices of the Peace living next the place where the party last of all, or lately then before dwelt, that he hath taken the Oaths of Supremacie, and Allegiance, and like Testimony from the Minister of the Parish of his conversation and conformity to the Orders and discipline of the Church of England. . . . And of these His Majesties Royall Commands, all the Officers and Ministers of His said Ports, and the Member thereof are to take care, as they will answer the neglect thereto at their perils."

country. Religion was one of the greatest sources of turmoil among the populations of Europe in the sixteenth and seventeenth centuries. Catholicism had been the predominant faith, and the Catholic Church a source of tremendous political power, for hundreds of years. But the Church was challenged by a group of people who became known as Protestants, who reinterpreted the Christian gospel and religious practices across Europe. Dozens of different Protestant sects appeared throughout the continent. Among these were the Puritans and the Society of Friends.

The Puritans were ardent reformers who felt that the Church of England (whose practitioners were called Anglicans) had retained too much of the pomp and ceremony of the Catholic Church. The Society of Friends, also known as Quakers, felt that spirituality was inherent in each person and that worship at formal church ceremonies was not necessary. Both the Puritans and the Quakers found themselves targets of persecution in England.

The Quakers were scorned by King Charles II, who in 1662 allowed Parliament to include them in the category of "Rogues and

Vagabonds." An act of Parliament recommended such individuals be banished from England, and many were deported to the New World. The statute was designed to prevent "the mischiefs and dangers that may arise by certain persons called Quakers, and others, refusing to take lawful oaths," such as swearing an oath in court. Refusal to do this would be met with "abjuration of the realm [removal of citizenship] or transportation to the Plantations."[20]

Fleeing Persecution

Many others departed willingly. Puritans left England for the New World in the 1630s and 1640s to escape the growing backlash against them. With the unspoken support of King Charles I, William Laud, the archbishop of Canterbury, was moving to enforce religious uniformity throughout England, Scotland, and Ireland as head of the newly established Commission for Regulating Plantations. Dissenters faced

A group of English men, women, and children known as Pilgrims depart from Europe. Fleeing religious persecution was a major reason many Europeans voyaged to the New World.

prison sentences and, in extreme cases, torture or execution if they refused to join the Anglican Church. Laud's efforts ended when he was removed from the commission in 1641, but the persecution of dissenters in England continued.

Citizens of other nations were also subject to discrimination because of their beliefs. The religious change that swept through Europe in the sixteenth and seventeenth centuries meant hardship for those who worshipped differently from the official church of the land. In France, which was officially Catholic, Protestants were called Huguenots. Throughout this period, the Huguenots were seen as a problem by France's kings. Some kings were willing to tolerate them, while others wanted to force them to return to Catholicism under penalty of death. But others felt that the best way to rid themselves of these dissenters was to offer them passage to the New World.

However, as the French government was unwilling to sponsor Huguenot colonies, French dissenters were "forced to seek refuge in the lands and colonies of rival powers,"[21] primarily those of England.

England Welcomes the Persecuted

By the time the flood of Huguenots began to flee religious persecution in France, Spanish colonists were concentrated in Central and South America, with a number of outposts in what is now California, Arizona, and New Mexico. These colonies, under Spanish Catholic rule, did not appeal to Protestants. English colonies had also spread across a wide area of the New World from Newfoundland to South Carolina. These colonies had greater appeal to Huguenot families. The English government had actively encouraged foreign Protestants to voyage to the New World since 1666. The government felt this would strengthen its colonies while diminishing Spanish colonial influence. In 1681 Charles II proclaimed that all Protestants were welcome in the English colonies, inviting

> such afflicted Protestants, who, by reasons of the rigours and severitys which are used towards them upon the account of their religion, shall be forced to quitt their native country, and shall desire to shelter themselves under his Majestys Royall protection for the preservacon and free exercise of their religion.[22]

In the New World, they would have the freedom to "follow commerce, arts, and trades as permitted by the laws of the realm."[23] This outreach was so successful that an estimated forty thousand to fifty thousand French Huguenots sought refuge under the English crown.

With each Huguenot family, Puritan follower, or Quaker dissenter that reached the New World colonies and lived to speak of the colony's advantages, more people in the colonists' homelands began to think about what the New World held for them. News of these foreign lands, and the initial successes of the new colonies there, drove many to seek a new life in the New World.

Preparing to Leave

Once the prospective emigrants had decided to leave, they had a number of tasks to accomplish. First, they had to select a ship for the voyage. Then they accumulated all the necessary supplies. Next, these supplies and household goods were transported by wagon

F. Delfinum

A sixteenth-century painting depicts the landing of French Huguenots in South Carolina. Some French kings allowed dissenters to depart for the New World.

to the port from which the emigrants would embark. Everyone's supplies were loaded aboard the chosen ship. Finally, the passengers needed to board the ship before it could be ready to sail.

These tasks could take weeks or months, and involved working with friends, family, and skilled tradespeople to ensure everything was ready when the time came to leave. Some families and individuals chose to wait until they reached their port of embarkation to assemble the necessary goods, often subjecting themselves to unscrupulous merchants charging high prices for the necessary goods. Oth-

ers tried to have everything ready for the voyage before they left their homes.

Food for the Voyage and Beyond

Perhaps the most important part of the preparation was the gathering of foodstuffs. Each wave of English settlers learned from the last, and each voyage was better supplied than the one before. For example, the Reverend Francis Higginson left England in 1630 for the Massachusetts Bay Colony. That same year in London, he published a pamphlet that laid out in great detail what the prospective colonist should bring. Reminding his readers that the new colonists must be prepared to subsist on what they brought along for up to a year, until a homestead could be developed and the first crops harvested, he advised bringing "8 Bushels of meale, 2 Bushels of Pease, 2 Bushels of Oatemeale . . . 2 Gallons of Vinegar . . . also Cheese, Bacon, Sugar, Pepper, Cloves, Mace, Cinnamon, Nutmegs and Fruit."[24]

However, John Josselyn, who traveled to Boston a few years later and recorded his own thoughts for prospective emigrants, advised that some items were better bought in the New World. He suggested that while spices were still important to bring along, "your best way is to buy your Sugar there, for it is cheapest."[25] It was up to each voyager to decide which advice to follow.

Men and women in rural areas grew as much food as they could and frequented local markets to buy the other foodstuffs they needed, accumulating them as quickly as pos-

sible to reduce the chance of spoilage. Then the foodstuffs had to be readied for the ocean voyage. Meat was preserved through drying, smoking, or salt curing. Some fruits and vegetables were also dried, but a significant portion of the food for the voyage itself was kept fresh. Once it was prepared, the food had to be packed for the voyage; the voyagers hired a cooper to make barrels for storage, to ensure the food would not spoil en route.

Household Goods

The household items needed in the New World were part of everyday life for many families. Pots, pans, utensils, and wooden trays for eating, called trenchers, were already present in most emigrants' homes. If a new kettle or skillet was needed, the family hired a local blacksmith to have it made before the voyage.

One of the most time-consuming matters was assembling clothing for the journey. Extra clothing had to be made for each member of

---

What a Ship Provided and What Passengers Should Provide Themselves

William Wood, in his 1634 pamphlet *New-Englands Prospect* (reprinted in George Francis Dow's book, *Everyday Life in the Massachussetts Bay Colony*), wrote that some ships included provisions for their passengers for the Atlantic crossing, but that it was to the travelers' advantage to ensure that they brought some provisions of their own as well:

"[Ships generally provide such foods as] salt Beefe, Porke, salt Fish, Butter, Cheese, Pease, Pottage [stew], Water-grewell [oat-

meal], and such kind of Victualls, with good Biskits, and six-shilling Beere; yet it will be necessary to carry some comfortable refreshing of fresh victuall. At first, for such as have ability, some Conserves, . . . Sallat-oyle likewise, Prunes are good to be stewed: Sugar for many things: White Biskits, and Egs, and Bacon, Rice, Poultry, and some weather-sheepe to Kill aboard the Ship: and fine flower-baked meates, will keep about a weeke or nine days at Sea. Juice of Lemons well put up, is good either to prevent or curre the Scurvy."

In this illustration, a group of Pilgrims prays before their New World voyage aboard the Mayflower *in 1620.*

the family, and this task fell to the women of the family. Mothers taught daughters the necessary steps for making cloth from natural products such as sheep's wool or a woody plant called flax. The girls learned how to card, comb, and spin wool into cloth; how to harvest and prepare the flax plants' fibers for weaving into linen; and how to cut and sew the cloth into clothing. One writer advised that each member of the family be provided with "a long coarse coate" for the voyage "to keep better [clothes] from the pitched ropes and plankes"[26] of the ship. Bedding and blankets were also needed. The same writer advised that, aboard ship, its quality did not matter as long as it was clean and warm.

With all the goods assembled for their new life, the emigrants arrived at their port of embarkation, ready to leave for the New World. But in many cases, there was a substantial waiting period before their voyage began. Sometimes this was because of the weather or the season; sometimes it was due to delays in outfitting the ship.

Timing Is Everything

During the height of the emigration from Europe in the 1600s, shipping businesses were busy throughout the year collecting cargo, repairing and outfitting existing ships, building new ships, and signing up passengers. Northern European mariners and emigrants alike understood that the best time of the year to depart across the North Atlantic was in late spring, and shipping businesses worked hard to have their ships ready by that time. Both the ships' owners and the captains wished several ships to sail together for safety, and departures were often delayed until all the ships were ready. One correspondent in 1638 mentioned that fourteen ships at a time could be found in the Thames River near London, preparing for the crossing.

For the passengers, therefore, securing passage on a ship and arriving at the port on time did not always mean that their journey would begin as planned. Instead, they often found that one or more ships was not fully prepared for the voyage. This forced them to find lodging in whatever quarters they could afford, while their goods joined the other waiting emigrants' supplies on the town's docks. It might be weeks before the passengers could board the ship and their goods could be loaded.

Boarding the Ship

The individuals departing for the New World discovered that each captain had a particular routine about loading his ship. In general, cargo was loaded first, with heavier items placed deep in the hold. This helped stabilize the ship in rough weather. Crews also had to load a variety of livestock such as cattle and sheep. These were also placed as deep in the hold as possible, although sometimes smaller animals, such as chickens, were loaded in cages and secured to the top deck.

Sometimes merchants' supplies that were being shipped to the colonies were loaded before the passengers and their essential chests containing food, clothing, and tools. According to researcher Mary N. Ganter,

Unfortunately, the priorities of captains and merchants were seldom in accord

with those of their passengers. Ships' masters loaded their vessels with merchandise and emigrants first, and then took on as much baggage as would fit. Often the vital chests were loaded onto other ships or left behind altogether.[27]

Once on board, other circumstances delayed the emigrants' departure.

Delays Aboard Ship

Delays could take place after the passengers had boarded the ship but before they had set sail. Weather conditions sometimes delayed ships' departure from port. A small storm by modern standards could keep seventeenth-century sailing ships bottled in a port for days until the winds shifted and the seas subsided. Delays once emigrants had boarded ship often had future consequences. According to Ganter, "sailing dates were notoriously unreliable, and emigrants forced to wait in the wind, weather, or whim of the captain consumed a substantial portion of their rations before the voyage began."[28]

In addition, one final detail often delayed the departure of English emigrants. Sometimes it took place as the passengers boarded in ports such as London or Dover; other times it took place at the last town the ship visited in the west of England before heading across the Atlantic. The last detail was the oath of allegiance. Without it, an English emigrant could not legally leave for the New World.

Taking the Oath

One of the lingering effects of Laud's campaign for religious uniformity was the oath of supremacy and allegiance to the Church of

England. Each passenger needed to affirm that he or she would remain a loyal subject to the English crown, and each ship's captain was required to carry a record of these oaths on board ship.

Ships' records from the seventeenth century affirmed that they sailed "with certificates from the ministers where [the emigrants] last dwelt, of their conversation, and conformity to the orders and discipline of the church, and they had taken the oath of allegiance and supremacy."[29] With this last detail out of the way, the passengers could begin their voyage.

Departing

In the sixteenth and seventeenth centuries, emigrants bound for the New World left from a variety of European ports. Spanish colonists left Seville for colonies in the Caribbean and Central and South America. Dutch settlers left Rotterdam bound for the New Netherland colony on the Hudson River in what is today New York and New Jersey. Swedish settlers left Gottenburg bound for the Delaware River valley of today's Delaware, New Jersey, and Pennsylvania. French religious dissenters and Catholics alike departed from Brest or Le Havre; the Huguenots bound for Acadia, which is today Nova Scotia, and the Catholics headed for the settlements of today's Quebec and Newfoundland.

Additionally, English emigrants left London, Southampton, Bristol, Dover, and other seaports headed for a variety of destinations in America, such as the New England settlements in the Massachusetts Bay Colony, the Plymouth Bay Colony, and Connecticut. They traveled to the Chesapeake Bay colonies of

Reverend Francis Higginson's Advice

The Reverend Francis Higginson immigrated to the Massachusetts Bay Colony in 1630 and became the first minister in the new settlement of Salem. In this excerpt from *Every Day Life in the Massachusetts Bay Colony*, he gives advice about what the prospective immigrant should bring with him to the New World:

"Before you come, be careful to be strongly instructed what things are fittest to bring with you for your more comfortable passage at sea, as for your husbandry occasions when you come to the land. For when you are once parted with England you shall meete neither markets nor fayres to buy what you want. Therefore be sure to furnish yourself with things fitting to be had before you come: as meale for bread, malt for drinke, woolen and linen cloath, and leather for shoes, and all manner of carpenters tools, and a great deal of iron and steele to make nails, and locks for houses, and furniture for ploughs and carts, and glasse for windows, and many other things which were better for you to think of there than to want them here."

Virginia and Maryland, and they also crossed the Atlantic to Rhode Island, a haven for even the most outspoken religious reformers.

A quick sea passage meant about fifty days at sea; some emigrants were three months upon the Atlantic before making landfall. And for many, the voyage became a defining moment in their lives, as it marked the end of what they had always known and the beginning of the unknown.

Daily Life on a Voyage to the New World

Regardless of the nationality, religious beliefs, marital status, or family size of the immigrants who undertook a voyage to the New World in the sixteenth and seventeenth centuries, they all shared the common experience of crossing the Atlantic. They established daily routines of food preparation and cooking, caring for their livestock, practicing their religion, and entertaining their children.

Ships of the Sixteenth and Seventeenth Centuries

Each voyager crossed the ocean on a sailing vessel built of wood and controlled by the brute strength of its crew. But none of these ships was intended primarily for the immigrants' voyage. The wooden sailing vessels that crossed the Atlantic Ocean in the sixteenth and seventeenth centuries were generally designed for carrying cargo, not passengers, to and from the colonies. These ships were built with wide hulls; mariners today would call them "wide in the beam" or "beamy." This design allowed a ship to carry as much cargo as possible while remaining manageable by the system of sails and rigging used during that period.

Many of these ships would seem small by modern standards. Historian Roger Daniels wrote that, to modern eyes,

the ships seem incredibly tiny. Some were only forty feet in length—shorter than a city bus!—although the average in the

seventeenth century was probably twice that. . . . John Josselyn came over on a large ship that carried 164 passengers. They and a crew shared less than fifteen hundred square feet of deck space—less than ten square feet per person—and a hold barely high enough for a man to stand erect in.[30]

These were the sorts of vessels upon which thousands of immigrants embarked to sail to the New World.

Accommodations on Board

Emigrant ships of the seventeenth century typically had two decks between the top deck and the hold. There were also small enclosed spaces built atop the top deck at the bow (front; rhymes with "now") and the stern (rear) of the ship. These small areas typically held living quarters.

The crew occupied the area at the bow, called the forecastle (which can also be spelled fo'c'sle, and is pronounced "FOKE-sull"); it was a common area where the crew built bunks or slung hammocks from the ceiling. In the stern were private accommodations occupied by the captain and his officers. But the passengers were confined to the areas below the main deck. A cutaway drawing of a typical English vessel from 1655 describes each deck as having six-and-a-half-foot clearance. Although people were generally shorter in that era (a six-foot-tall individual was considered unusual), this did not give the passengers much headroom. Passengers were expected to spend the majority of their trip to the New World within these spaces.

Dark, Damp, and Stifling

The decks were dark, damp, and poorly ventilated. Portholes—small openings in the ship's hull—were little more than wooden flaps that could be raised outward in good weather and calm seas. They provided a bit of light and ventilation to the area immediately around them, but did little to alleviate the stifling atmosphere of the passengers' quarters. They were generally kept closed, as water from even moderate seas could pour in through them.

Some ships were equipped with hatches on the main deck, which, when opened, helped provide ventilation to the areas belowdecks. These were also usually kept closed, however, because of the danger from high seas. Other

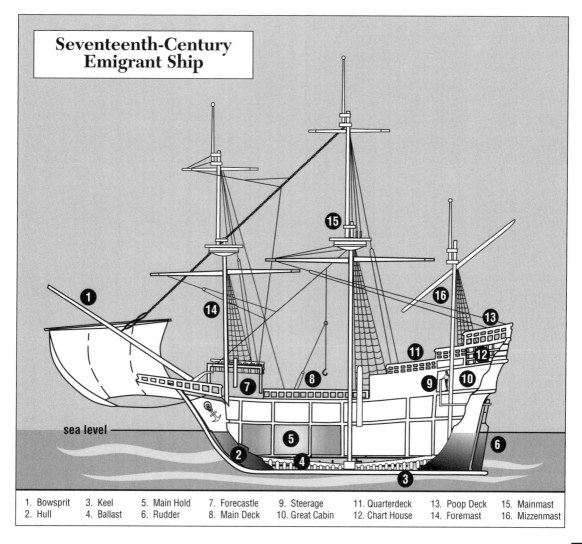

Seventeenth-Century Emigrant Ship

sea level

1. Bowsprit	3. Keel	5. Main Hold	7. Forecastle	9. Steerage	11. Quarterdeck	13. Poop Deck	15. Mainmast
2. Hull	4. Ballast	6. Rudder	8. Main Deck	10. Great Cabin	12. Chart House	14. Foremast	16. Mizzenmast

ships had gratings, which were openings in the decks covered by wood lattice. These allowed more light and ventilation into the areas belowdecks, but they could also be a safety hazard. The English emigrant John Winthrop recorded an incident that pointed out the dangers of these hatches: "A maid of Sir Richard Saltonstall fell down at the grating by the cook-room, but the carpenter's man, who occasioned her fall unwittingly, caught hold of her with incredible nimbleness, and saved her, otherwise she had fallen into the hold."[31]

In addition to the lack of ventilation, the areas belowdecks were relatively cold, even in the heat of summer, as they were cooled by the temperature of the chilly ocean waters of the North Atlantic surrounding the ship. They were undoubtedly foul smelling, as the odors of dozens of unwashed bodies mingled with the smells of the livestock and their dung from the hold below. They were also likely to be noisy; the combination of the creaking of the ship, the wind and the waves, and the sounds of the tethered cattle and horses in the hold must have been quite a combination during rough weather. Historian Alan Taylor writes that breaks from this monotony were infrequent: "Only in relatively calm weather, and only for a few hours a day, could the passengers partake of the fresh air and distant views from the deck. Most of the time they huddled below as the pitching vessel churned through the cold and stormy waters."[32]

Accommodating Families

The emigrant ships were filled with a variety of people venturing across the Atlantic. Voyages to the New World were made by individuals of all ages, and families with young children were a significant part of this migra-tion. For example, the biographer of emigrant William Ward noted that "several of the settlers brought families of fair size—from five to nine children of all ages. Ward had five children . . . : John, the oldest, being in 1638 about twelve years of age; Joanna ten; Obadiah six; Richard three; and little Deborah, one."[33]

Traditionally, sailors were used to living with men and were unaccustomed to having women and children on board. Some ship captains and crews felt that the easiest way to accommodate these emigrants was to house them in separate areas belowdecks. Consequently, once aboard ship, the passengers sometimes found themselves separated from their family members and acquaintances for the majority of the voyage.

Sleeping Arrangements

Adding to the discomfort first felt by the emigrants as they faced life belowdecks was the assignment of sleeping arrangements. The spaces provided for sleeping were often nothing more than boxes built into the sides of the ship, stacked two or three high, with a small passageway between them along the center of the deck. They were built to accommodate as many as four people across, but were too closely built atop one another for anyone to be able to sit up, and they were too open to be considered private.

On such voyages, individuals were assigned a berth by the captain. Family groups might find themselves split up for no apparent reason. According to Ganter, "Single men and women might be assigned to share a wide berth with a married couple. Some women preferred to spend the nights sitting up on a box to the alternative of sleeping under the same blanket with a strange man."[34]

Pilgrim families pray together before boarding the Mayflower. *Aboard ship, women and children were typically housed in separate quarters from the men.*

Creating Daily Routines

The enclosed spaces; the cold, damp, and foul air; the lurching of the ship; and the fatigue caused by poor sleep wreaked havoc on many passengers. To occupy their time and to keep up their spirits, enterprising voyagers established a number of shipboard routines for the duration of the voyage. These helped them take their minds off the difficult conditions.

Any daily routines developed by the passengers had to take place out of the way of the sailors, as each watch of the crew was busy with its own routine while the ship was in motion. For these passengers, survival was tied to the condition of their food supplies. Fresh-

water, fruit, and vegetables played an important role in their diet, but fresh meat was considered essential. The care and feeding of the animals that the passengers had aboard ship was a vital part of the emigrants' daily routine.

Caring for Animals

It was not difficult for the emigrants to care for small animals such as chickens and pigs, which were often kept in cages on the main deck. The animals could be fed and their cages cleaned with relative ease in good weather.

However, the large animals in the hold, such as horses and cattle, were harder to reach and to maintain. Taking care of such animals on land requires hard work; aboard ship, it was much more difficult. The animals were generally unaccustomed to being kept in enclosed spaces for weeks on end. It required special patience and devotion to keep the animals calm; if agitated, these animals could injure themselves or the emigrants by kicking or thrashing about in panic.

On a daily basis, these animals required large amounts of hay for food, and they created large amounts of waste. In the best circumstances, when the ship had smooth sailing in calm weather, the passengers could change some or all of the straw to keep the areas clean, tossing the dirty straw overboard. But despite the passengers' best efforts, the straw bedding in the animals' spaces eventually became soiled and began to reek. Additionally, the passengers were forbidden to leave their own quarters during rough seas. In extreme cases, the animals might go days without food or water. Keeping all the animals on board in good health was an important task for the emigrants, because healthy animals were better able to endure the journey, and provided higher quality meat when chosen for consumption.

Food Preparation

One of the first, and one of the most important, routines to establish on the ship was food preparation. It is likely that food preparation took up a good deal of the day for the passengers, their servants, and the ship's cook and his assistants.

Animals carried aboard the ship supplemented a diet of preserved foods such as hardtack and salted beef. Each animal that was intended to be eaten on board had to be slaughtered and the meat prepared for cook-

The Diary of John Winthrop

John Winthrop, who was one of the leading Puritans in the New World, kept a diary of his voyage to the New World in 1630. This excerpt records part of the passengers' routine during the Atlantic crossing:

"Sunday, 11 April, 1630: The wind at N and by W a very stiff gale. . . . In this time (which hindered us five or six leagues [fifteen or eighteen miles]) the *Jewel* and the *Ambrose* came foul of each other, so as we much feared the issue, but, through God's mercy, they came well off again, only the *Jewel* had her foresail torn, and one of her anchors broken. This occasion, and the sickness of our minister and people, put us all out of order this day, so as we could have no sermons.

Monday, 12 April, 1630: The wind more large to the N a stiff gale, with fair weather. In the afternoon less wind, and our people began to grow well again. Our children and others, that were sick, and lay groaning in the cabins, we fetched out, and having stretched a rope from the steerage to the mainmast, we made them stand, some of one side and some of the other, and sway it up and down till they were warm, and by this means they soon grew well and merry."

ing. Aboard ship, however, using sharp knives and cleavers for killing and cutting up animals into pieces for cooking could be a difficult task, as the deck pitched and heaved beneath them. No doubt accidents occurred until the preparers became accustomed to the conditions.

Puritan leader John Winthrop and his crew stand on the deck of the Arabella *off the shore of Salem, Massachusetts, in 1630.*

To supplement food supplies aboard ship, the crew often hunted a variety of sea turtles, including the Hawksbill turtle (pictured).

Occasionally, the crew sighted a school of fish or other marine life, and the crew and passengers attempted to catch it with nets. These catches helped augment the diet on board. One voyager mentioned a large array of food caught while his ship was under way, including Spanish mackerel, shark, and a variety of sea turtles, which he found to be especially good eating:

> Of the Sea Turtles there be [four] sorts, first the Trunck-turtle which is the biggest, Secondly, the Loggerhead-turtle. Thirdly, the Hawkbill-turtle, which with its bill will bite horribly. Fourthly, the Green-turtle which is best for food, it is affirmed that the feeding upon this turtle for a twelve moneth, forebearing all other kind of food will cure absolutely Consumptions [tuberculosis], and the great pox [syphilis].[35]

After the animals were slaughtered and prepared for cooking, they were taken to the ship's hearth on the top deck.

Cooking

The cooking hearth was a center of activity throughout an Atlantic voyage. Some hearths, constructed of bricks, were open on one side so the cooking fire could be maintained. Over each hearth was an iron tripod, from which kettles of varying sizes could be hung. Other ships had a more primitive setup, in which barrels were lined with bricks to contain the cooking fire, and covered with grills on which food was placed.

According to Ganter, a member of the crew was sometimes put in charge of cooking for the entire ship, "but the catch was that the cook had to be bribed with cash or liquor.

Some passengers got five hot meals a day, while others got one, maybe every other day."[36]

Cooking for a crew of thirty-five to fifty men was a full-time occupation for a cook. Adding another hundred tired, cold, listless, and bored emigrant passengers would have been too much for one man to handle. Consequently, on some ships, the passengers were left to fend for themselves. Sharing the hearth with other individuals or other families could be either a source of entertainment or a point of contention. Families might share ingredients for meals or they might squabble over whose turn it was to use the hearth. If the cooking facilities were insufficient for the number of voyagers aboard, scuffles often broke out over access to the fires.

All sorts of foodstuffs went into the kettles or onto the grills at mealtime. A variety of concoctions, such as stews, roasts, and soups, came out. Each depended on what the passengers had on board, what the ship was providing, and, in some cases, what they caught along the way.

In the best of circumstances, there were enough hearths to accommodate passengers and crew, enough freshwater in which to boil meat or fish, and enough firewood to keep fires going for as long as they were needed. However, there were other circumstances that kept the passengers and crew from cooking and eating.

Fasting

Not all voyagers were able to augment their hardtack and salted beef with catches from the sea. In some cases, the supply of food provided by the ship—which was supposed to be enough for a three-month voyage—ran out long before the crossing was completed. William Bradford, in his *History of Plimoth*

Plantation, recalled the fate of one ship that was shipwrecked off Cape Cod, Massachusetts, in the dead of winter. According to Bradford, the unfortunate passengers "had been 6 weeks at sea, and had no water, nor beere, nor any wood left, but had burnt up all their empty caske"[37] in order to survive.

Additionally, there were times when no cooking could take place. If the ship was caught in a storm or was battling rough seas, all the passengers were kept below, out of the way of the crew. Without access to the hearths, the emigrants had to get by with cold food. On one voyage, a diarist noted a strong storm that blew from the west-southwest for three days. The storm not only virtually halted the ship's progress toward the New World, it also kept the passengers from cooking for almost three days. One day's note read in the margin, "Fast. In the great cabin, at nine at night, etc., and the next day again, etc. The storm continued all this night."[38]

Once the storm had passed, the captain gave permission to the passengers to return to their regular routines. The emigrants eagerly took advantage of this opportunity to cook fresh food and to air out the areas belowdecks—and, with the captain's approval, to venture up on deck for some fresh air.

Time up on Deck

Perhaps the most beneficial routine in the emigrants' daily lives was being allowed up on deck. They did not have the opportunity every day, so they were quite enthusiastic at the chance to venture out into the sunshine and the sea breeze.

Passengers of all ages were allowed to walk about the deck and to get some exercise. Such activity certainly energized the passengers and improved their outlook on the voyage. It also likely helped to restore an appetite that might have been dormant for several days or more, and they could look forward to eating again. Winthrop's diary recorded one such beneficial day:

> This day the ship heaved and set more than before, yet we had but few sick, and of these such as came up upon the deck, and stirred themselves, were presently well again; therefore our captain set our children and young men to some harmless exercises, which the seamen were very active in, and did our people much good, though they would sometimes play the wags [act the fool] with them.[39]

On this ship, the emigrants and crew interacted quite well, but that was not always the case.

Interaction with the Crew

Undoubtedly, these emigrants were the subject of discussion among the mariners. The ship's master and crew likely did not interpret their faith the same way as the passengers. By and large, according to Roger Daniels, "most seamen were at best indifferent to their passengers and at worst, downright hostile."[40] One diarist noted the death of a crew member, "a most profane fellow, and one who was very injurious to the passengers, though much against the will of the master."[41]

It is unknown whether this crewman injured the passengers verbally or physically. Although his opinions might have reflected those of his fellow countrymen, the ship's master apparently understood that it was to the crew's advantage to keep their views to themselves. Tolerance of a particular group could bring more of that group's business

A Salute to Voyagers

When the first colonists departed England to establish what became the Jamestown colony in Virginia, musicians performed a ballad on shore as the ships left the docks. This merry ballad by Michael Drayton is quoted in Samuel Eliot Morison's *The Oxford History of the American People:*

"Britains, you stay too long,
Quickly aboard bestow you,
And with a merry gale,
Swell your stretched sayle,
With vows as strong
As the winds that blow you.

And cheerfully at sea,
Successe you still intice,
To get the pearle and gold,
And ours to hold,
Virginia,
Earth's only Paradise."

their way. In any case, it seems that his behavior tested the patience of some of the emigrants.

Religion Aboard Ship

For many of the Europeans who crossed the Atlantic, the trials of an ocean voyage in a wooden sailing ship tested their faith. Emigrants who shared the same faith established routines for worship that lasted throughout the voyage.

Surviving journals note days of worship and moments set aside for prayer. These moments of devotion ranged from expressions of thanks spoken at meals to group worship activities conducted by one of the emigrants' leaders. They were often held in the passenger spaces, but could also be held up on deck if the weather permitted and the captain felt they would not interfere with the crew's routines.

In some cases, passengers chose to forgo food, creating a "fast day." For some religious dissenters, fasting was a common occurrence, used in conjunction with a day of prayer for a specific desire. For example, these individu-

als might undertake a day of fasting and prayer to ask God for peaceful seas or the birth of a healthy child. Fasting aboard ship could be seen as a test of one's faith or as an offering.

George Fox, a Society of Friends leader who joined a number of emigrants on a voyage in 1671, recorded in his diary how the passengers commemorated escaping an encounter with a suspected pirate ship:

A Puritan minister preaches to a group of passengers on deck. Many emigrants established strict routines for religious worship during their voyage.

Nine-Men's Morris

According to Masters Traditional Games Ltd. (www.mastersgames.com), nine-men's morris is an ancient board game for two players, each with nine pieces.

"The game . . . is played on a board consisting of three concentric squares connected by lines from the middle of each of the inner square's sides to the middle of the corresponding outer square's side. Pieces are played on the corner points and on the points where lines intersect so there are 24 playable points. . . . The basic aim of the game is to make "mills"—vertical or horizontal lines of three in a row. Every time this is achieved, an opponent's piece is removed, the overall objective being to reduce the number of opponent's pieces to less than three or to render the opponent unable to play. To begin with the board is empty.

Players take turns to play a piece of their own color on any unoccupied point until all eighteen pieces have been played. After that, play continues alternately but each turn consists of a player moving one piece along a line to an adjacent point.

Whenever a player achieves a mill, that player immediately removes from the board one piece belonging to the opponent that does not form part of a mill. If all the opponent's pieces form mills then an exception is made and the player is allowed to remove any piece. Captured pieces are never replayed onto the board and remain captured for the remainder of the game. The game is finished when a player loses either by being reduced to two pieces or by being unable to move."

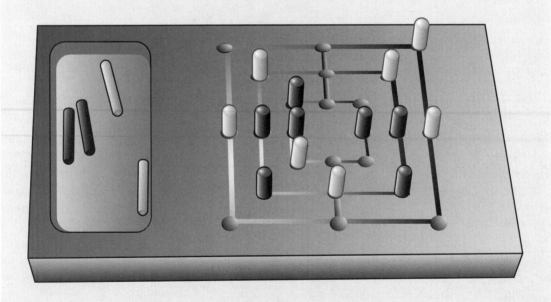

The next day, being the first day of the week, we had a public meeting [for worship] in the ship, as we usually had on that day throughout the voyage, and the Lord's presence was greatly among us. I desired the people to remember the mercies of the Lord, who had delivered them; for they might have been all in the [pirates'] hands by that time, had not the Lord's hand saved them.[42]

Fox's proclamation was undoubtedly similar to other declarations of deliverance made throughout the emigration period. The emigrants, many buoyed by their faith, saw the completion of each day at sea as a sign that their voyage was blessed. And at the end of the day, they might find time to amuse themselves and their children with a game or a story.

Games and Diversions

It is important to remember that children of all ages were making the journey, along with family servants as young as ten or twelve. If the voyage was difficult for the adults, it was even more so for the young. Frightened children needed something to do to pass the time. Mothers and fathers worked to help the children learn about the voyage, and the ship, and to keep them occupied.

Young children are easily bored with their surroundings. The restlessness of these emigrant children was made more intense by continual confinement to the area belowdecks. However, during the seventeenth century, children over the age of six or seven were treated as small adults, and were expected to act accordingly. According to writer Anuradha Kumar, "most would have spent much of their time working with their parents (and thus learning the skills they would need in later life), but they also found time to play. . . . Many of the board and dice games would have been equally popular among children as adults."[43]

Some of the popular games for both children and adults of the period included backgammon and nine-men's morris; the patterns of these board games were often carved into a barrel top and game tokens were easily made from any scraps of wood that might be at hand. Among some emigrant groups, such as the Puritans, card games were frowned upon. To them, card games were at best a waste of time and taught nothing; at worst, they were a means to gamble, which was considered a sin. Chess was popular because it was considered a game that taught logic and strategy, and challenged one's mind.

The passengers also passed the time by telling stories. Some were allegorical, and they were often based on tales from the Bible. They were designed to teach a lesson to the listeners, giving advice on how to behave and how to deal with difficult situations. Others were oral histories—tales of the homeland they had left behind, or the adventures of their ancestors. The most successful storyteller could occupy fellow passengers for hours, as the ship churned across the Atlantic, and took the listeners' minds off the hardships of the voyage. For a time, at least, they were unconcerned with the challenges and hazards of the journey.

However, as the crossing continued, many unforeseen hazards awaited the passengers and crew. Whether man-made or natural dangers, each tested the will of the men, women, and children aboard ship.

Hardship, Danger, and Death

CHAPTER 4

Little could prepare the emigrants for life aboard an ocean vessel at sea. Regardless of the routines established by the passengers and crew they still had to deal with a number of unexpected and uncontrollable factors, such as seasickness, contagious diseases, poor diet, and piracy.

One of the greatest unknowns over which they had no control was the sea itself. Even when the weather cooperated and seas were fairly calm, the open, rolling sea was a new experience, and storms at sea could turn their new experience into a nightmarish one. Tales of the dangers of the sea were widespread among mariners and nonmariners alike; the Reverend Francis Higginson wrote of one "sore and terrible storme" when "the wind blew mightily, the rayne fell vehemently, the sea roared & the waves tossed us horribly; besides it was fearfull dark & the mariners . . . was afraid."[44]

Storms at Sea

Crossing the Atlantic Ocean in a sailing vessel required constant vigilance and preparedness on the part of the ship's officers and crew. They were accustomed to reading the waves, the clouds, and the wind, and were prepared to make any necessary changes to deal with an oncoming storm.

For example, changes in the direction or the speed of the wind meant changes in the weather; a rising wind usually forecast in-clement weather. Clouds that appeared to cover the horizon and an increase in the size of the waves signaled an approaching storm. Whether or not that storm would reach the ship remained to be seen.

Sudden wind shifts or velocity changes could catch the men off guard, damaging the sails and the rigging. If sails were torn along a seam or ripped from the rigging, precious time was lost while repairs were made. While captains were accustomed to sailing into the prevailing winds, storm-generated winds could come from any direction, and their force could wreak havoc with a ship.

As a storm approached, wind gusts might reach seventy-five miles per hour. A ship's captain would order the crew to shorten sail, or reduce the sails to a minimum. Sails on all but the mainmast might be dropped and removed to the deck. Even so, the force of the wind on the masts and the rigging without sails (known as bare poles) could still damage a ship. John Winthrop recorded one such event during a storm:

> The wind SSW a good gale and fair weather, so we stood W and by N four or five leagues a watch, all this day. The wind increased, and was a great storm all the night. About midnight our [sister ship] put forth two lights, whereby we knew that some mischance had befallen her. We answered her with two lights again, and [sailed] up to her, so near as we durst, (for the sea went very high . . .) and hav-

ing hailed her, we thought she had sprung a leak; but she had broken some of her shrouds; so we went a little ahead of her, and, bringing our foresail aback stays, we stayed [nearby] for her, and, about two hours after, she filled her sails, and we stood our course together, but our captain went not to rest till four of the clock, and some others of us slept but little that night.[45]

With the repairs to the other ship completed—in the middle of the night, and in heavy seas—both ships were able to continue on.

"Man the Pumps!"

When a ship sprung a leak, the officers might call on the passengers for assistance in dealing

A fleet of ships sails over stormy seas. Storm-generated winds and rough seas often caused extensive damage to sails and hulls.

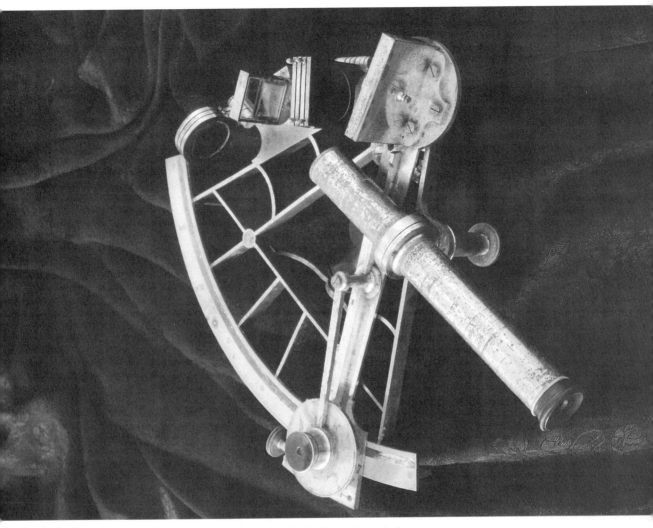

After a storm had passed, the crew determined the ship's latitude by measuring the angle of the sun or North Star using an instrument called a sextant.

with the situation. The most able-bodied of the emigrant men were selected to perform a variety of duties to help the ship weather the storm, such as manning the pumps in the hold.

This could be backbreaking work. The pumps were operated manually with wooden bars that were raised and lowered to create suction, which drove the water out of the hold through pipes and then dumped it overboard.

Men were assigned to man the pumps for hours on end, as the storm occupied the rest of the crew. In some cases, ships leaked no matter what conditions existed. Fox noted that, even in the best weather, his ship was "very leaky, so that the seamen and some of the passengers did, for the most part, pump day and night. One day they observed that in two hours' time she sucked in sixteen inches of water in the well."[46]

All aboard understood that this was an essential duty for the survival of the ship. Too much water in the hold not only made the ship heavier (and therefore more difficult to sail) and threatened the integrity of the ship's hull, but also threatened their possessions, their livestock, and perhaps their lives.

In fact, the combination of crashing waves and water entering the hold sank many ships. One Portuguese captain recalled an Atlantic storm that caught two ships in its fury. The crashing waves drove goods loaded on the top decks overboard, dismasted one ship, and so battered the other that it broke apart and sank without any survivors.

After a storm had passed, the officers and crew attempted to determine where they were. They determined their latitude as earlier mariners did, taking a sighting from the sun or the North Star, using an instrument called a sextant.

They also assessed the seaworthiness of the ship. If no pressing repairs were needed to areas above deck, the emigrants were allowed to venture outside. They caught up on a variety of important tasks, such as cooking and airing out bedding. Waves crashing over the ship drove water through closed hatches, and water leaked in around portholes or through pitched seams, adding to the passengers' discomfort during their confinement belowdecks. Clothing and blankets grew damp and were subject to mildew. The emigrants were eager to air out their spaces and their possessions as soon as possible.

Additionally, they took the opportunity to clean out the sleeping quarters. This was particularly important as some individuals had difficulty tolerating the heaving, shifting, tossing, and turning of the ship, combined with enclosed spaces and the cold, damp, and foul air. It is no wonder that seasickness was rampant, sometimes even before the ship left port.

Seasickness

Many of these passengers had never been aboard a ship before, much less one that was being tossed and turned by the wind and the waves during a storm. For them, the experience could be anything from mildly annoying to exceptionally terrifying.

Compounding the misery of these passengers was that belowdecks it was impossible to tell what was going on outside. The motion of a ship was easier to understand and tolerate when one had a point of reference, such as a mast on a heaving deck. But below among the weary passengers, seasickness spread quickly as the sounds of one person being sick only encouraged another's stomach churning.

Given these experiences, it is not surprising that some writers advised that, emigrants bring along something that could help settle their seasickness. Early Massachusetts emigrant William Wood advised that passengers provide themselves with "good Clarret Wine to burne at Sea; Or you may have it by some of your Vintners or Wine-Coopers burned here [in London], & put into Vessels, which will keep much better than other burnt Wine, it is a very comfortable thing for the stomacke, or such as are Sea-sicke."[47]

Seasickness was a mild health problem compared to the diseases voyagers faced. Smallpox, measles, and tuberculosis, common in European communities in the 1600s, were unknowingly brought on board by passengers and crew. These diseases soon claimed new victims, particularly among those already weakened by dehydration and hunger.

Contagious Diseases

Contagious diseases claimed far more victims in the 1600s than they do today. Vaccinations,

Smallpox

According to the Dittrick Medical History Center of Cleveland's Case Western Reserve University, a smallpox victim in the 1600s had the disease long before symptoms became apparent. The smallpox victim was infected usually through inhaling the virus.

"Most infections were caused by contact with someone who had already developed the characteristic skin lesions (pox) of the disease, from contaminated air droplets, and even from objects used by another smallpox victim (books, blankets, utensils). . . . After the virus entered the body, there was a 12–14 day incubation period, although no symptoms would be apparent. After incubation, symptoms appeared abruptly and included fever and chills, muscle aches, and a flat, reddish purple rash on the chest, abdomen, and back. These symptoms lasted about three days, and then the rash faded and the fever dropped. A day or two later, fever would return, along with a bumpy rash starting on the feet, hands, and face. The rash progressed, ultimately reaching the chest, abdomen, and back. The individual bumps (papules) would fill with clear fluid, and eventually become pus-filled over the course of 10–12 days."

treatments, and cures were far in the future; the first effective vaccinations against smallpox, for example, did not appear until the 1790s. And because these diseases were so common among the European population, emigrants expected, feared, and were resigned to the presence of the diseases on board their ships. Neurologist D.P. Lyle, who also specializes in the history of medicine, comments that "in a closed environment such as a ship at sea, panic and terror would be the rule of the day"[48] when smallpox appeared.

Smallpox was a fearsome disease that was spread easily through the air. Undoubtedly, passengers felt apprehensive at the first sight of the pustules and blisters that marked the disease. However, by the time the symptoms appeared, the disease was running full force through the victim. Smallpox was fatal for about one-third of those who contracted it. In the seventeenth century, it affected adults more than children.

One voyager noted the first case of smallpox on his ship. On his 1638 voyage, John Josselyn wrote, "and now a Servant of one of the passengers sickened of the small pox."[49] He and his fellow passengers had been aboard ship less than ten days, and were still in sight of England. The servant died ten days later, on May 11. Four days later, Josselyn wrote that smallpox was spreading through the ship. On June 16 he noted that "another lad"—who worked for the captain—had died during the night. But smallpox was not the only contagious disease with which the emigrants had to contend.

Other diseases such as measles and tuberculosis could be spread throughout a ship by just one infected passenger or crewman. Tuberculosis, like smallpox, was spread through the air when an infected individual coughed or sneezed. It progressed very slowly over a number of years, usually led to fever, cough, difficulty breathing, and inflammation, eventually infecting the lungs and other organs. In many cases, individuals died of dehydration, diarrhea, and chronic wasting of the body, as victims were unable to ingest and retain enough nutrients to survive, or suffocated due to lung damage.

Measles was less likely to spread through the air, but could be spread by infected passengers who sneezed or coughed onto a fellow emigrant. Symptoms such as a runny nose and a high fever appeared in as little as ten days, followed by a red rash that began at the hairline and spread over the entire body. In some cases patients experienced convulsions, deafness, and swelling of the brain. Pneumonia often accompanied the outbreak and caused the largest number of deaths from the disease.

Scurvy, Dysentery, and Malnutrition

Contagious diseases were not the only health risks that were present among voyagers to the New World. Noncontagious conditions such as scurvy and malnutrition were probably as common as contagious ones aboard ship. Scurvy—a vitamin C deficiency that can lead to joint pain and tooth loss in the early stages, and blindness and death in severe cases—was just becoming understood in the seventeenth

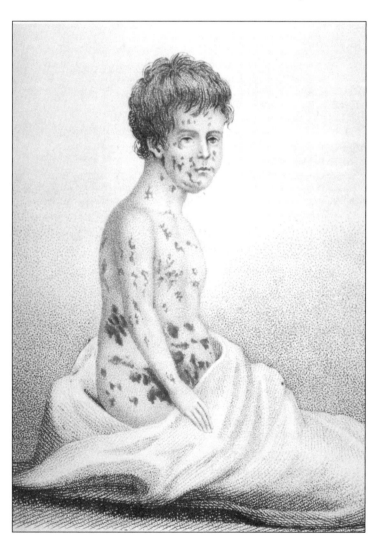

An illustration shows a young boy suffering from smallpox, an extremely contagious disease that claimed the lives of many New World voyagers.

century. Keen scientific observers had noticed that those who ate fresh foods were less inclined to scurvy, especially on long ocean voyages, and travelers were advised to bring fresh fruit with them on the voyage. In fact, fresh fruit was such a valuable commodity that it was often kept under lock and key. On one voyage, one of the captain's servants was publicly whipped on deck for stealing and eating nine lemons.

As the voyage wore on and the supply of fresh meat, fruit, and vegetables was diminished or exhausted, both crew and emigrants began to suffer from malnutrition, which can be caused by the lack of a single vitamin in the diet, from not eating enough food, or from the inability to digest food properly.

Additionally, freshwater quickly grew stale, especially in warm weather, making it unpalatable. The water supplies easily became contaminated by microorganisms present in the water before the voyage began and from sources such as hands and utensils that were improperly cleaned. Drinking water that was contaminated led to dysentery. Eating food contaminated through contact with uncooked animal juices or unclean hands and utensils could cause it as well. The victim's intestines became infected, leading to stomach pains, fever, vomiting, diarrhea, and sometimes death. The disease spread not only through the contaminated food supply, but also from contact with an infected individual.

Death at Sea

For those unfortunate individuals who contracted a disease such as smallpox or dysentery, there was often little their companions

---

The Arrival of John Josselyn

In 1638 English adventurer John Josselyn completed his first voyage to the New World. In his *Account of Two Voyages to New-England*, he records a variety of shipboard activities as well as navigational landmarks as they made landfall in June:

"The Fourteenth day of *June*, very foggie weather, we sailed by an Island of Ice . . . three leagues in length mountain high, in form of land, with Bayes and Capes like high clift land, and a River pouring off it into the Sea. . . . These Islands of Ice are congealed in the North, and brought down in the springtime with the Current to the banks on this side *New-found-land*, and there stopt, where they dissolve at last to water. . . . Here it was as cold as in the middle of January in En-gland, and so continued till we were some leagues from it. . . .

The Two and twentieth, another passenger died of a Consumption [tuberculosis]. Now we passed by the Southern part of *New-found-land*, within sight of it. . . .

The Nine and twentieth day . . . now we are two leagues off *Cape Ann* [Massachusetts]. . . .

July the first day, we . . . descried land.

The Third day, we anchored in the *Bay* of *Massachusetts* before *Boston*. Mr. *Tinges* other man now dyed of the small pox. The tenth day, I went a shore upon *Noddles Island* to Mr. *Samuel Maverick* ([who paid] for my passage) the only hospitable man in all the Countrey, giving entertainment to all Comers *gratis*."

A nineteenth-century painting depicts the burial at sea of Sir Francis Drake in 1596. Most passengers who died at sea were buried with little or no ceremony.

could do to help them get better. The best they could do was to make the ill person as comfortable as possible, and members of the religious groups who made the voyage to the New World took the opportunity to pray for the individual's health.

If the victim died, the captain and crew were informed, as they were essential in dealing with the dead body. In a few cases the captain might permit a funeral ceremony, but according to the surviving records of the time, many individuals were buried at sea with little or no ceremony. For example, the first victim of smallpox on John Josselyn's ship had weights tied to his neck and legs and was "turned out at a Port-hole."[50]

A burial at sea was a time-honored practice for those who died at sea, and the transatlantic mariners carried on this tradition for themselves and their passengers. On a practical note, the burial prevented the spread of disease; if a victim died of smallpox, a burial at sea removed the risk of further infection from the corpse. Additionally, sixteenth- and seventeenth-century mariners had no way to preserve a body for later burial until they reached land, which could be months away.

Birth at Sea

Sometimes a death among one's shipmates was countered by a birth. From surviving written accounts of emigrant voyages, it is apparent that many families opted to make the voyage even though their groups included women who were six months or more pregnant. It is likely that the presence of one or more pregnant women meant that someone on board the ship, or at least on board one of the other ships in the fleet, had some training in childbirth delivery techniques. While some ships had doctors on board, a midwife and other women with children of their own were more helpful in this situation. John Winthrop mentioned that one of the women on his ship, the *Arabella*, "fell in travail, and we sent and had a midwife out of the *Jewel*. She was so far ahead of us at this time, (though usually we could spare her some sail,) as we shot off a piece and lowered our topsails, and then she brailed her sails and stayed for us."[51]

With the onset of labor, this woman had the support of other women among the voyagers. They kept the other passengers out of the sleeping area, or, if the captain was accommodating, moved her to the officers' quarters for more privacy. In the best of circumstances, the ship was in relatively calm seas, with pitching and rolling at a minimum. Aboard the *Arabella*, the wind was "full S and towards night a good gale. We stood W and by N,"[52] meaning that the ship was sailing northwest under a southerly wind of fifteen to twenty-five miles per hour. This would have sent the ship rolling from side to side while the woman was in labor.

The winds increased the next day and shifted to the south-southwest as the ship continued northwest; now the ship would also have been pitching forward and backward, like a seesaw. Lying on a bunk, the woman held onto the sides for support; the other women in the room tried to keep their footing in the rolling seas; and the midwife concentrated on both the health of her patient and the movement of the deck. But the midwife could do little to help the woman's labor, and in fact, some common practices of the day actually lengthened the labor. According to Lyle, the common practice of administering alcohol lessened the force of the woman's contractions "with the net effect of prolonging the mother's ordeal."[53] As far as is known, the woman aboard the *Arabella* gave birth successfully, and mother and child survived the rest of the voyage.

This child, as well as untold others born during transatlantic voyages, was brought into an uncertain world. Beyond the small world of the ship crossing the ocean, and the unknowns of the nature of the sea, European nations were vying for dominance in the New World.

Additional colonial efforts meant greater numbers of ships on the Atlantic with supplies for, and goods from, the New World. These ships became tempting targets for outlaws, and the possibility of contact with these outlaws often affected the outlook of those on board the emigrant ships crossing the ocean.

Pirates

Pirates were an emerging threat to sea trade. These pirates came from many areas. Many were from North Africa, from the ports in what is today Morocco, Algeria, and Tunisia, but were generally referred to as "Turks" by the northern Europeans. The pirates, who were originally concentrated in the Mediterranean Sea, eventually spread out into the eastern Atlantic and sailed up and down the

Privateering and the Lost Colony

A group of colonists left England in 1587, intending to start a settlement on the shores of the Chesapeake Bay. But for reasons that remain a mystery, they ended up at the site of England's previous colonial attempts— today's Roanoke Island, North Carolina. All that survives of the written record from that venture is the official account of their leader, John White, from July 22, 1587, in which he firmly places the blame on Simon Ferdinando, the fleet's pilot.

"But assoone as we were put with our pinnesse from the ship, a Gentleman by the meanes of Ferdinando, who was appointed to returne for England, called to the sailers in the pinnesse, charging them not to bring any of the planters [colonists] backe againe, but to leave them in the [Roanoke] Island, except the Governour [White], and two or three such as he approved, saying that the Summer was farre spent, wherefore hee would land the planters in no other place. Unto this were all the saylers, both in the pinnesse, and shippe, perswaded by [Ferdinando], wherefore it booted not the Governour to contend with them, but passed to Roanoak, and the same night at sunneset went aland on the Island."

Historians theorize that White claimed that Ferdinando had subverted the expedition's goals. White believed Ferdinando had convinced the officers and crew of the other ships to leave the colonists at Roanoke and to then sail to the Caribbean. There they could prey upon Spanish ships and return to England with the bounty. It would be far more profitable than the colonial expedition.

European coast. Pirates also came from England, France, and the Netherlands. They preyed on ships that were smaller or less heavily armed than they were, regardless of the ship's origin or destination, taking the cargo and the ship, and occasionally taking the crew and passengers hostage as well.

Popular tales of the day regaled listeners with deeds of pirates and their lawless ways. Tales of renegades with swords, muskets, and pistols who tortured and marooned unfortunate members of trading vessels resonated throughout the period of New World emigration. Both ships' captains and the emigrants aboard ship feared that they could be attacked by pirates. Thus, it was prudent for each emigrant ship that crossed the Atlantic to be armed against pirates, from whatever source.

Protecting Against Dangers from Abroad

Each male aboard an emigrant ship was expected to have some sort of weapon, such as a dagger or a sword, or, if he was well-to-do, a firearm such as a musket or pistol. Not only would the weapon be needed in the New World for hunting and defense, it would also come in handy if the ship was attacked. The captain and crew tested each man to see how skilled he was with his weapon and how he could be incorporated into the crew's defensive tactics. Winthrop wrote that while his ship was still in English waters near the Isle of Man, "Our captain called over our landsmen [male passengers], and tried them at their muskets, and such as were good shot among them were enrolled to serve in the ship, if occasion should be."[54]

Any ship encountered at sea was subject to suspicion. During the age of sail, each ship's lookout was responsible for looking for sails on the horizon and alerting the officer of the watch. Sighting an unexpected ship—especially one that seemed to be heading toward one's own ship—was cause for alarm.

George Fox's diary recorded an encounter with an unknown ship. As word spread through the ship of the other vessel, the crew and the passengers began to fear that the newcomer was filled with Turkish pirates. The ship seemed to be heading straight for Fox's ship, no matter what maneuvers the crew made to escape it. Fortunately, a gale arose during the night, and the accompanying wind and heavy rain hid them from the other ship. Fox wrote, "we sailed briskly on and saw them no more."[55]

Passengers and crew aboard an emigrant ship had good cause to be wary of an approaching vessel. In addition to pirates of unknown origin, the threat sometimes came from one's fellow countrymen.

Impressment

Naval vessels of all nations occasionally stopped civilian ships at sea. Emigrant ships were boarded by national naval officers, who were empowered to take any man they chose

Pirates typically preyed on small, poorly armed ships. In this eighteenth-century painting, a band of pirates attacks a captain and his crew.

"The Lowlands of Holland"

In the mid–seventeenth century, England and the Netherlands were involved in a number of wars over maritime commerce and colonial expansion. During each conflict, the English navy needed men to fill its ships, and sent press gangs to find them—whether they wanted to join the navy or not.

From this time period comes a ballad called "The Lowlands of Holland," which records a lover's lament at her new husband's becoming pressed.

"On the night that I was married and on my marriage bed
There came a bold sea captain and he stood at my bedhead
Crying, 'Oh, rise oh rise, young married a man, and come along with me
To the low lowlands of Holland, to fight your enemy.'

Oh I held me love all in my arms still thinking he might stay
But the captain he gave another order, he was forced to march away.
Crying, 'There's many a blithe young married a man this night must go with me
To the low lowlands of Holland, to fight the enemy.'

Oh Holland is a wondrous place and in it grows much green
'Tis a wild inhabitation for me true love to be in
Where the grass do grow and the warm winds do blow and there's fruit on every tree
But the low lowlands of Holland parted me love and me.

No shoe no stocking I'll put on no comb go through my hair
Nor shall no coal nor candlelight shine in my bower fair
Nor will I lie with any young man until the day I die
For the low lowlands of Holland parted me love and I."

through a practice called impressment. Impressment was the practice of forcibly enlisting one or more men in naval service, regardless of who or where they were—even if the men were from another country. This sometimes happened while the ship was in home waters or still in port. "Press gangs" often roamed seaside ports, rounding up men and boys and presenting them to the nearest naval vessel in return for a bounty for each man selected.

Impressment was a cause for concern for emigrants as they sailed to the New World in the second half of the 1600s. Men could be separated from their families with little or no cause. Naval officers were restricted from pressing an entire crew, although sometimes they came close to doing so. Legally, they were supposed to leave the ship with enough crew members to sail the ship home, but naval officers and ships' captains often disagreed about the number of men required to safely sail a ship. The naval officers felt it took fewer men than the captains claimed, and usually ignored the captains' protests. In 1671 George Fox and his shipmates encountered a pressing before they left England:

Before we could sail, there being two of the King's frigates riding in the Downs, the captain of one of them sent his press-master on board us, who took three of our seamen. This would certainly have delayed, if not wholly prevented, our voyage, had not the captain of the other frigate, being informed of the leakiness of our vessel, and the length of our voyage, in compassion and much civility, spared us two of his own men.[56]

When the civilian ship was cleared to set sail, the passengers discovered that with a reduced crew on board, the character of the voyage had changed. Fewer crew members meant the voyage would likely take longer than expected to complete. A reduced crew meant there were fewer hands to man the sails, to handle the ship in a storm, and to deal with emergency situations such as manning the pumps. More of the male emigrants were requested to help with daily routines, and as the voyage dragged on, more and more of the men—both passengers and crew—fell victim to fatigue, injury, and disease.

With the potential dangers of diseases, storms at sea, and piracy present throughout the period of emigration to the New World, it is a wonder that men and women chose to brave the voyage. But during the 1600s, hundreds of thousands Europeans emigrated from England, France, Spain, the Netherlands and other countries to the New World; from England alone, 350,000 crossed the Atlantic. They sought a new life across the seas, and they were willing to take a chance on a voyage fraught with potential danger and hardship. However, they were not the only people to make the journey. Untold thousands of others made the same journey quite unwillingly, and faced an even more uncertain future in the New World.

Unwilling Emigrants

During the seventeenth century, thousands of unwilling emigrants—men, women, and children native to Africa—crossed the Atlantic. They were taken from their homelands by force; held captive and sold as property to strangers who, to them, looked and acted strangely; and herded onto ships for a nightmarish voyage across an environment completely alien to them. And once their journey ended, they were forced into a lifetime of slavery in the New World.

The Need for Cheap Labor

Before the rise of African slavery in the New World, much of the labor in the colonies was performed by indentured servants. An indentured servant was a man or a woman who was willing to work for an individual for a period of time, usually five to seven years, in exchange for a bonus such as land at the end of that time. In the case of the New World voyagers, someone in the servant's home country or in the colonies would pay for the servant's fare and supplies in exchange for his or her labor once he or she arrived in the New World.

Indentured servitude was common in the agricultural Chesapeake colonies of Maryland and Virginia. There, widely scattered plantations grew commodities such as tobacco and corn for export, and each plantation required a labor source to plant, tend, and harvest the crops.

The indentured servants were an inexpensive source of labor for the landowners, but once a servant had fulfilled the contract term, he or she was free to leave the plantation. The completed contract cost the former

Servants to the New World

In *The Oxford History of the American People*, historian Samuel Eliot Morison describes the character of the servants who voyaged to the New World colonies:

"'Servant' in the colonial era meant about the same as employee in ours; and within the class there was as wide a variation as today between migrant farm laborer in California and a master electrician. In the English and Dutch colonies, a servant was usually a person whose passage was paid, or assisted, in return for working a certain number of years—usually four or five as an adult, more for a minor. . . . This system of exchanging the cost of passage and outfit for a few years' labor was the principal means of peopling the English colonies. . . .

Servants . . . might be of any class, from poor gentlemen to convicted felon. The average servant was a respectable young person who wished to better himself in the New World but could not afford the cost of outfit and passage."

*African slaves are brought to shore in the New World. Throughout the
seventeenth century, thousands of African slaves were brought to the New World.*

The First Africans in Jamestown

In her article "'In the Service of Several Planters': Virginia's Early Africans," Nancy D. Egloff records how the Africans mentioned by John Rolfe in 1619 came to Virginia on a Dutch ship:

"While studying records in Seville, Spain, historian Engel Sluiter learned that these Africans were slaves on their way from Africa to Spain's colonies in the New World . . . when the Dutch ship stole them. The Spanish, however, were not transporting them. Rather, Spain had an agreement with merchants from the country of Portugal, who took the slaves in Africa and then shipped them to Spain's colonies. The 20-plus Africans were from the Portuguese colony of Angola on the west coast of Africa.

Another historian, John Thornton, has researched what life was like for these men and women in Africa. Many were from Ndongo, an area of palisaded towns, with each town having about 5,000 thatched houses. The people grew food crops of millet and sorghum, tended herds of cattle, and raised goats, chickens, and guinea fowl. . . .

The 1619 Africans came from a small area of Angola, probably spoke a common language, and had similar cultural practices. They also had years of experience trading with Europeans and were probably able to adapt better to life in Virginia than later groups that did not have similar backgrounds. In addition, because of recent wars in West Africa, many people had already been enslaved by Africans, and then by the Portuguese."

In other words, these Africans were already slaves on their way from Africa to the Caribbean when the Dutch ship stole them.

---

employer not only the price of the bonus, but also a seasoned employee. Additionally, improving economic conditions in England in the mid-1600s meant fewer individuals chose indentured servitude as a means of getting ahead. So plantation owners were in continual need of a labor source that was inexpensive and constant. They found it in the enslavement of Africans.

The First Slaves Arrive in the Chesapeake

It is difficult for historians, some four hundred years later, to assess exactly what happened on these slave voyages. It is also difficult to ascertain how many Africans came to the New World to work for the Spanish and Portuguese in Central and South America in the 1500s. But it is easier to determine when the first slaves came to the English colonies in the New World. In fact, a planter in Jamestown, Virginia, noted it in his diary.

John Rolfe recorded various events that took place in the colony. In 1619 he wrote, "About the last of August came in a dutch man of warre [ship] that sold us twenty Negars."[57] This comment is seen by some historians as the beginning of African slavery in the English colonies.

The Virginia and Maryland planters soon realized that although these Africans, purchased as slaves, were more expensive in the short term than European indentured servants, the Africans were bound to servitude for life. There were no promises of freedom after seven years and no promises of land bounties or business opportunities. In short, it made better economic sense to the Europeans to use African slaves rather than European servants to do their work.

That is not to say that the Chesapeake planters were the only ones who saw it this way. Africans were enslaved throughout the New World by settlers from every European nation: on Massachusetts farms, in New Netherland households, on Portuguese plantations in Brazil, and in Spanish mines in the Caribbean and South America. Europeans throughout the New World imported slaves, forcing men, women, and children to voyage to the New World from their African homelands.

Coastal Trading Factories

During the initial years of trade the Dutch, Portuguese, and English established fortified trading posts in Africa. As the slave trade grew, these coastal trading stations grew and eventually became known as factories, under the direction of a man called a factor. On the coast of Africa, trading factories became a one-stop supply depot for European ships. According to historian Donald R. Wright, these factories grew up

> on western Africa's small islands, riverbanks, or ocean beaches [where European trading companies] had slaves "bulked," awaiting purchase and shipment for the New World. Slaving vessels could appear; purchase slaves on hand; obtain food, water and firewood; and be off within a short time for American markets.[58]

The slaves arrived at the factories from far and wide, often at the end of a long forced march from the interior. One eyewitness recalled that the slaves

> are commonly secured, by putting the right leg of one, and the left of another,

A slave is whipped outside an open-air enclosure where dozens of slaves are confined as they await the arrival of the slave ship.

into the same pair of fetters [iron bands]. By supporting the fetters with a string, they can walk, very slowly. Every four slaves are likewise fastened together through the necks, with a strong rope of twisted thongs; and in the night, an additional pair of fetters is put on their hands, and sometimes a light iron chain is passed around their necks.[59]

By the time the prisoners arrived at the coastal factories, they were physically and mentally exhausted. Although their arrival at the coastal factory meant the end of the march, it was only the beginning of their difficult journey to the New World. If no ships awaited them, they waited at the factory. In some cases, they were confined to an open-air stockade, much like a livestock pen. In other cases, they were forced to spend time inside a barracoon.

Inside the Barracoons

A barracoon was a building inside or outside the factory's fortifications that was used to confine slaves. These buildings were not built for comfort. There was almost no privacy inside the barracoons. At some factories, men and women were placed in the same rooms inside these structures; at others, they were separated. The buildings were usually dark and poorly ventilated, with no bathroom facilities. Chained to the walls, men and women relieved themselves where they were, fouling the dirt floors and soiling their clothing. The barracoons were stiflingly hot during the heat of the day and chilly during the night.

Throughout the days and nights, as their captors awaited the next slave ship's arrival, the men and women sat inside, with little ability to move their cramped muscles. They had had little time to recover their strength after the long journey to the coast, and now they were merely trying to survive on the meager diet of local produce, such as corn or yams, that they were provided.

According to historian William D. Piersen, when they conversed with the other occupants, "talk too often revolved around rumors that the prisoners were going to be sold to hideously repulsive foreigners"[60] who would carry them off across the western sea. It was inside the barracoons that the men and women began to realize that their life was about to change drastically. The arrival of the slave ship was yet another shock.

The Arrival of the Strangers

The slave ships that arrived at the coastal trading factories were unlike any vessels that most of these Africans had ever seen, and the ships were manned by people who were utterly foreign to them. According to researcher Joseph C. Miller, tales of horror circulated among the people of what is today the African nation of Angola, who "feared the whites' intention of converting Africans' brain into cheese or rending the fat of African bodies into cooking oil, as well as burning their bodies for gunpowder."[61] As individuals from their group were pulled from the barracoon or the stockade and presented to the newcomers, murmurs of fear and apprehension rippled through those left behind. To them, it seemed that the whispered rumors about strangers carrying their victims to the lands of cannibals were coming true.

Inspection and Selection

When a slave was brought in front of the European strangers, he or she was forced to

Slave owners inspect slaves for purchase at a slave market in Zanzibar. After purchasing slaves, the owner typically had them branded with a hot iron.

stand still for an inspection by the slavers. A cursory glance at the individual's physique was followed by poking and prodding of various parts of the body to test muscles and forcing open the mouth to check the condition of the teeth. Good teeth usually meant a healthy individual; missing or rotting teeth meant the opposite.

Men and women alike were stripped to ensure that the slave dealer was hiding nothing, such as a deformed foot or an early pregnancy. Those who were selected by the strangers were taken aside and, according to historian Alan Taylor, "received the trader's brand with a hot iron, searing their new status as property into the flesh."[62] Depending on the purchaser, the slave might be branded on the shoulder, the breast, or the upper arm. Some underwent the torture twice—once to signify the company that had purchased them, and a second time with the royal coat of arms of the purchaser's country.

After the last slave was branded, the slaver and the dealer finalized their prices. Piersen points out that for the African dealers, "in the 1680s a male slave could be traded for 17 guns on the western coast; at that time the value of 17 trade muskets was roughly equivalent to six times the yearly cost of living for a common man."[63] Meanwhile, the ship's crew took the bound and shackled men and women to the slave ship.

Boarding the Ship

European slave ships often employed a different sort of mariner than the emigrant ships of the same time period. While emigrant ships' crews may have been uncouth or condescending to the passengers, this behavior was generally discouraged by the captain and the ship owners; such behavior was bad for business.

The crews of slave ships had no such concerns, however, and the captains and owners would hire almost anyone for the voyages. Their behavior toward the slaves mattered little; after all, to them, the slaves were merely cargo. According to Piersen, "On the loading of the slaves, [the crew] would stand on deck rudely calling out their foulest thoughts as the women passed before them naked, shivering and terrified."[64]

Men, women, and children were kept chained until they reached the ship. Generally, once on board, the women and children were unchained, but the men were not. The slavers, believing the male slaves presented a greater threat to the safety of the ship and the crew, kept them restrained.

In most cases, slave ships called at several factories along the West African coast during a voyage. Therefore, it was not unusual for a newly purchased group of slaves to board a ship and discover that other Africans were already aboard, also in captivity. Hearing the moans and cries from the others belowdecks, smelling the stench from humans enclosed in small spaces in a tropical environment, or seeing the downcast faces of those who were already on the top deck in chains likely added to the newcomers' misery and depression. Soon the newcomers were forced down below the top deck and into cramped spaces where they would begin the Middle Passage: the Atlantic crossing to the New World.

The Middle Passage

There are many variables involved with voyages from Africa to the New World, called the Middle Passage because it represented the second of three legs of a ship's voyage from (and to) Europe. The treatment of the human cargo varied from ship to ship and from crew to crew. But it is possible to establish some basic elements of these journeys.

The space belowdecks where the slaves began their journey gave them perhaps half the space of those New World emigrants who made the trip of their own free will. Slave decks were usually only four or five feet high.

An often-reproduced image of the eighteenth-century slave ship *Brookes* shows men and women packed like spoons in a drawer, but this is an extreme case. Many slavers chose not to pack the slaves so tightly, and many captains apparently did not take on as many slaves as originally planned. However, the conditions the slaves endured during the Middle Passage were undoubtedly brutal and inhumane compared to those experienced by willing emigrants.

But the slaves were not confined to these spaces for the entire journey. According to Wright, "Captains kept Africans topside throughout the much of the day as weather permitted."[65] The captains realized that bringing the slaves on deck kept them in better health, which meant that more of them would survive to reach the New World. It also

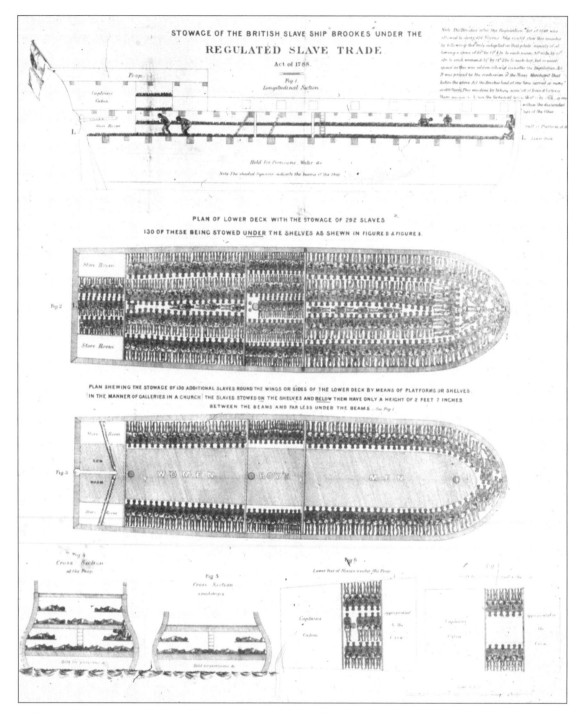

A diagram of the stowage of the eighteenth-century slave ship
Brookes *illustrates slaves packed like sardines in the lower decks of*
the ship.

gave the crew a chance to try to clean the decks where the slaves were kept, usually by washing them with a mixture of vinegar and seawater. And while the slaves were on deck, they generally received their meals.

Diet Aboard Ship

European slave traders discovered that slaves survived best on a diet of food from their native lands, although they sometimes supplemented these foods with hardtack or beans. French vessels purchased dried turtle meat in the Cape Verde Islands and fresh vegetables along the African coasts, to which oats were added to create stews. Portuguese ships stocked up on yams for the voyage, and English ships issued meals featuring peas and oatmeal.

These meals were hardly much more than what was required to keep the slaves healthy enough for their eventual resale in the New World. French captain Jean Barbot claimed that it was difficult to carry the large amount of yams for the slaves on a typical ship because the yams "take up so much room," but that it was necessary, as the slaves were "of such a constitution that no other food will keep them [alive]."[66] But many captains felt that the ships' owners had overestimated the amount of food needed for the slaves, or thought it was almost impossible to store the full amount aboard ship. In those cases, space designed for food storage was used for additional slaves. Consequently, each slaving voyage was susceptible to food and water shortages, as well as outbreaks of disease and personal injuries.

Dangers of Injury

Injuries aboard slave vessels were extremely common. Male slaves were continuously chained at the feet and the hands—sometimes to another slave, sometimes to the platform on which they were forced to sit or lie—and these heavy iron chains were a constant source of irritation on their bare skin. When the men were brought up on deck, these restrictive bindings became the cause of even more injuries.

Injuries came about when the slaving crew forced the slaves to exercise in a process called "dancing." The men and women were forced, through whippings, to jump about the top deck to the beat of an African drum or iron kettle, which was sometimes accompanied by a fiddle or a banjo played by a crew member. English captain Thomas Phillips recalled that "we often at sea in the evening would let the slaves come up into the sun to air themselves, and make them jump and dance for an hour or two to our bagpipes, harp and fiddle."[67] The exercise was somewhat beneficial, as it kept the slaves in good enough physical condition for their eventual sale. But at the same time, the practice was degrading, and the iron chains and shackles often rubbed the men's flesh raw until they bled. These wounds rarely had a chance to heal before the slaves were "danced" again. Broken bones likely resulted as men tried to favor one leg or arm over the other, more painful limb. In addition, these open sores were a prime target for infection.

Sometimes injuries resulted from beatings by the crew. Men were subjected to severe punishment for being uncooperative. Some slaves maintained their dignity despite their surroundings, refusing to become intimidated by the slavers regardless of verbal abuse and threats of punishment. But the crew often whipped these men and women to break down their resistance and to make an example of them for the rest of the slaves. The crew also used branding irons to

An eighteenth-century drawing shows a ship captain laughing sadistically as he tortures a female slave.

mark individuals seen as disruptive. Men and women who refused to eat were force-fed; the crew used hot coals to sear open their mouths and used funnels to pour food down their throats. Women were routinely raped and beaten; many did not survive their injuries.

In some cases, injuries occurred as a result of the rocking of the ship. For example, a sailing ship caught in a storm may be battered by wind and waves such that for hours on end the ship leans, or heels, over to one side. A ship assaulted by winds from the left, or port, side heels over to the right, or starboard side. Those slaves who were on the starboard side could be crushed by others who slid uncontrollably from the port side as the decks heaved. One Portuguese captain, recalling a storm that battered a slave ship, wrote that "it is then that the din from the slaves, chained to one another, becomes horrible. The clanking of the irons, the moans, the weeping, the cries. . . . Many slaves break their legs and their arms, while others die of suffocation."[68] In such circumstances, the ship's doctor could do almost nothing to mend broken ribs, punctured or collapsed lungs, or skull fractures. He was limited in what he could do by the supplies on hand as well as his own experience.

In such cases, the victims were carried quickly to the top deck once the storm passed. The doctor wished to remove the victim from the area because the doctor could withstand only a short time belowdecks before the stench drove him away. Additionally, doctors wanted to limit their own exposure to the slave decks for fear of contracting disease.

Dangers from Disease

As with willing emigrants to the New World, slave populations aboard ship suffered from a variety of diseases. Those with contagious ailments, such as smallpox and measles, infected others on the voyage. Other diseases, such as malaria and yellow fever, were African diseases that could not be transmitted from person to person. Malaria, which is spread by mosquito bites, infects an individual for life, and recurs frequently with fevers, chills, and nausea and vomiting. If untreated, the victim can suffer from a liver disease called jaundice and can die from anemia, a condi-

tion in which a lack of red blood cells can lead to heart failure or stroke. Yellow fever, also spread by mosquitoes, can lead to high fever, chills, headache, muscle aches, vomiting, and backache, and may lead to shock, bleeding, and kidney and liver failure.

Seasickness was also endemic among these people who had never been at sea. After a few days at sea, the slave decks were covered with vomit and human waste from individuals too weak to move, and although crews tried to wash the decks while the slaves were on the top deck, the filth was almost impossible to eliminate.

These were prime breeding grounds for disease. In addition, contaminated food and water contributed to the ill health of the slaves. This, of course, was not desirable from the point of view of the captain, as his profits for the voyage were directly related to the

An advertisement for a slave auction in Boston stresses that the slaves for sale are healthy and free from smallpox.

health of his human cargo. Yet the concern for the health and welfare of the cargo was in direct contrast to the general inhumane treatment of the men, women, and children in his charge.

Uprisings and Suicides

It is not surprising that some slaves revolted and tried to take over the ship. These uprisings were generally short lived; the unarmed and weakened Africans were quickly overpowered by the European crews. Many were killed in the resulting violence, but it seems that they preferred dying in a struggle for freedom to dying slowly from disease or maltreatment. Surviving leaders of the uprisings were, according to an eyewitness, "treated as villains" and were "punished to intimidate the rest"[69] by execution.

Many men, women, and children suffered from depression over their circumstances. They were overwhelmed by their inhumane treatment and by the prospect of being taken to a foreign land and enslaved. Some tried to commit suicide in order to escape the ship's hardships. One seventeenth-century French writer recorded that "some throw themselves into the sea, others hit their heads against the ship, others hold their breath to try to smother themselves, others still try to die of hunger from not eating."[70]

Some ships tried to prevent slaves from jumping overboard by tying nets around the outside of the ship. If a slave avoided the nets and reached the water, the captain sent crewmen in boats to retrieve the escapee. If the individual was brought back alive or survived the fall into the nets, he or she was usually put to death for trying to escape. Given these additional risk factors, it is not surprising that slave ships suffered an alarming mortality rate.

Death During the Middle Passage

While disease claimed many victims among willing immigrants to the New World, the death rates were even higher among slaves. Historian Phyllis Peres estimates that "some eleven to twelve million Africans were taken on ships for passage to the Americas between 1520 and 1860. Only nine to ten million survived the Atlantic crossing"[71] to reach the New World. Men, women, and children died from injuries, disease, and suicide.

Overall, mortality aboard a slave ship averaged about 20 percent during the seventeenth century. On some voyages it was higher, especially if the voyage took longer than expected and the food ran out or spoiled, or if storms or disease led to injuries or death. This means that on an average voyage with 250 slaves, 50 men, women, and children died. For those who survived their encounters with disease and violence, the end of the voyage was no reason to celebrate. Unlike those who voyaged to the New World willingly, their arrival in the New World meant only more hardship and sorrow.

The Arrival

From the day the first sailing ship left sight of land to venture to distant shores, sailors looked forward anxiously to sighting land again. Lookouts, posted high in the rigging, scanned the horizon for signs that they were approaching the shore, such as flocks of birds or cloud banks. They also watched the water, noticing changes in color that indicated that the sea was getting shallower—which meant that land might be nearby. And when they thought that what they were seeing did indeed indicate land, they cried out, "Land ho!" for all to hear.

Both mariners and passengers understood that such sightings were often misleading. Cloud banks often formed with no land beneath them; birds could be blown out to sea by storms. But at the cry of "Land ho!" the crew sprang into action to confirm the sighting. The captain and officers scanned the horizon themselves, with the aid of their spyglasses, and if they agreed with the lookout that, indeed, land had been sighted, the word spread quickly through the ship. It was a time for celebration for all, and one all remembered for the rest of their lives.

"I See the Land!"

Few firsthand records of these early arrivals in the New World have survived to this day. Official narratives of the voyages record the places visited and landmarks named, but tell little about the feelings of the individuals on board.

However, one valuable eyewitness record has survived since the fifteenth century. Diego Alvarez Chanca, who served as surgeon on Christopher Columbus's second voyage to the New World, left an account of the expedition and recorded the sailors' joy at sighting the modern island of Dominica in November 1493:

> On the first Sunday after All Saints, namely the third of November, about dawn, a pilot of the flagship cried out, "The reward, I see the land!"

> The joy of the people was so great, that it was wonderful to hear their cries and exclamations of pleasure; and they had good reason to be delighted; for they had become so wearied of bad living, and of working the water out of the ships, that all sighed most anxiously for land.[72]

Undoubtedly, sighting and reaching land—called "making landfall" by mariners—was a time for celebration for all aboard an ocean-going ship. For both passengers and crew, it meant that they would soon have an opportunity for fresh food and water on shore. For the passengers who had been stricken with bouts of seasickness throughout the voyage, it meant a chance to experience solid ground again. But at the same time, it also meant it was time for some hard questions. The most important question was, "Where are we?"

Celebrations and Questions

Many ships were trying to reach New England, which stretched from modern New Jersey (the northern limit of what the English called Virginia) to the coast of today's Maine. The mariner who had surveyed the coast and had given it its name claimed it was a land where "every man may be master of his own labour and land . . . and by industry grow rich."[73] In 1620 a group of emigrants left England upon the now-famous ship the *Mayflower* and headed to this rich and fertile land.

At first, the *Mayflower*'s passengers were overjoyed at reaching the New World. William Bradford, the chronicler of the voyage, wrote that the colonists "fell upon their knees and blessed the God of Heaven, who

Columbus and his crew rejoice at sighting land in the New World. Sighting land was a time for celebration for all aboard New World voyages.

had brought them over the vast and furious ocean, and delivered them from all the perils and miseries thereof, again to set their feet on the firm and stable earth, their proper element."[74]

However, many of the passengers were dismayed by the appearance of where they had actually landed. Bradford wrote:

> Being thus passed the vast ocean, and a sea of troubles . . . they had now no friends to welcome them, nor inns to entertaine or refresh their weatherbeaten bodys, no houses or much less townes to repair too. . . . it was muttered by some that if they had not got a place in time they would turn them and their goods ashore [and return to England].[75]

Arriving in the New World . . . Somewhere

Once an emigrant ship had made landfall, the challenge for the mariners was to match their observations of the newly sighted coastline with their charts and their own experiences. English, French, and Dutch fishermen who had explored the rich fishing grounds that today comprise the east coast of Canada and the New England states had the experience of navigating in the North Atlantic and had gained knowledge of coastal landmarks such as islands, bays, rivers, and hills. They passed this information on to their colleagues and to European mapmakers. Consequently, maps of these areas became more and more accurate.

As both charts and navigational experiences improved through repeated voyages, the answer to the question, "Where are we?" became more certain. However, knowing where the ship's first landfall was led to the question of how far it was from its destination.

The initial jubilation of the emigrants aboard the *Mayflower* over reaching the New World was quickly tempered by confusion about their landfall, which was on the shores of what is today Provincetown, in Cape Cod, Massachusetts. According to historian and essayist Alistair Cooke, "thanks to an incompetent navigator, the *Mayflower* missed even the northern limits of Virginia by a good two hundred miles."[76]

Within ten years of the *Mayflower*'s arrival in the New World, other English arrivals were more certain of their navigation and their landfall. Consequently, when the first Puritans voyaged to the New World, the mariners had a wealth of information about landmarks along the coast. John Winthrop and others on the *Arabella* first sighted land on June 8, 1630:

> The wind still W and by S, fair weather, but close and cold. We stood NNW with a stiff gale, and, about three in the afternoon, we had sight of land to the NW about ten leagues, which we supposed was the Isles of Monhegan, but it proved Mount Mansell.[77]

The *Arabella*'s charts of the coastline of the modern state of Maine were so accurate that Winthrop could confidently record that they had not landed at the Isle of Monhegan but rather at the Isle of Mount Mansell (now called Mount Desert Island), approximately sixty miles away. His journal continued:

> Then we tacked and stood WSW. We had now fair sunshine weather, and so pleasant a sweet air as did much refresh us, and there came a smell off the shore like the smell of a garden. There came a wild

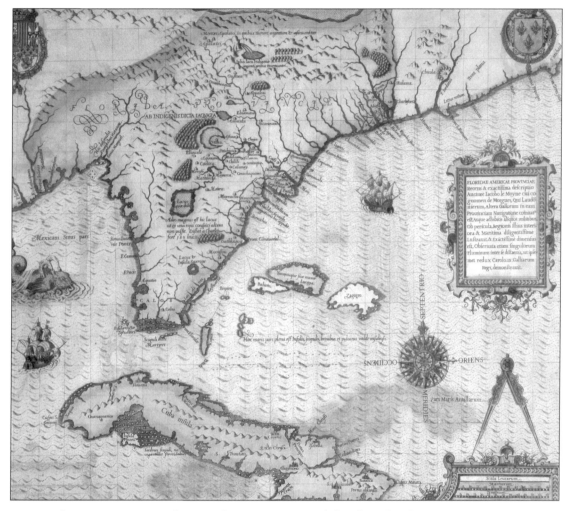

A sixteenth-century map provides a crude representation of Florida and Cuba. The accuracy of European maps increased with every New World voyage.

pigeon into our ship, and another small land bird.[78]

With the difficult Atlantic crossing now behind them, the emigrants now had to re-board their ship. No doubt some were thoroughly tired of being on board their ship, and would have been happy to disembark wherever they were in the New World. However, most emigrant ships were headed to a specific location, and those who were weary of the sea

had to endure it a bit longer before they could leave the ship for good.

Journeying to an Intended Destination

During the early days of emigrant journeys to the New World, this additional time at sea could amount to more than a week. For example, the first English colonists who crossed the Atlantic in 1587 took the southern route, making several stopovers at Spanish-held islands in the Caribbean, where they took on fresh food and water. They returned to their ships for an additional fifteen days before they reached Roanoke Island on North Carolina's Outer Banks. The first French attempt at colonization in today's United States also traveled via the southern route and made stops in Martinique and Antigua before continuing north to establish a short-lived colony in what is today Florida.

By the early 1600s, however, northern European ships avoided the southern route pioneered by Columbus in favor of braving the North Atlantic. English, French, Dutch, and Swedish ships reached the coasts of what is today Newfoundland or Maine first before traveling south to their final destination.

Even when travelers took the shorter northern route, the voyage could take just as long, especially if the emigrants were searching for new land to claim. For example, when Sweden considered establishing a colony in the New World, Swedish mariners consulted with Dutch mariners about a suitable location that was unclaimed by the English, Dutch, or Spanish. Peter Minuit, who had been involved with the Dutch settlements in New Netherland, led the first voyage of Swedish adventurers in 1638 across the North Atlantic and then south, past the New England and

The *Sea Venture*, Bermuda, and *The Tempest*

During the first few years of the English colony at Jamestown, Virginia, the colonists experienced hardship, hunger, and death, and relied upon supplies brought from England. Several fleets crossed the Atlantic to support the colony, and one, the so-called Third Supply Relief Fleet, sailed from Plymouth, England, in 1609.

The fleet was composed of eight ships: the *Diamond*, the *Blessing*, the *Falcon*, the *Unitie*, the *Lion*, the *Swallow*, the *Catch*, and the *Sea Venture*. On July 25 they were caught off the Azores Islands by an intense storm, possibly a hurricane. The *Catch* sank and all aboard perished; the fleet was scattered across the ocean for days, and when the storm abated, the *Sea Venture* was alone. William Strachey, who was aboard the *Sea Venture*, described his experience:

"A dreadful storme and hideous began to blow from out of the North-east, which swelling, and roaring as it were by fits, some houres with more violence than others, at length did beat out all light from heaven; which like an hell of darknesse turned black upon us."

The crew of the *Sea Venture* eventually discovered they were in the vicinity of the Bermuda Islands, and ran the ship ashore in order to make landfall. All those on board—almost 150—survived. They spent forty-two weeks on Bermuda, celebrating Christmas and building two small ships from the remains of the *Sea Venture*, and sailed on to Jamestown in 1610.

The other ships of the fleet had arrived months earlier and the *Sea Venture* had been given up for lost, so the arrival of the ships from Bermuda was met with great celebration. Their shipwreck and survival led to the first permanent settlement on Bermuda, and their story, widely told in England, may have been an inspiration for William Shakespeare's play *The Tempest*.

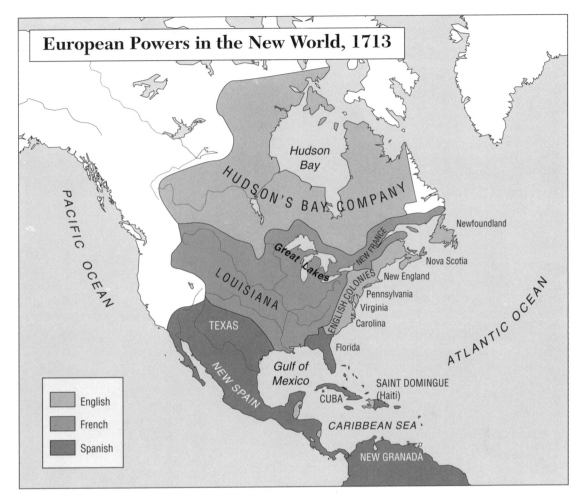

European Powers in the New World, 1713

Hudson Bay

HUDSON'S BAY COMPANY

Newfoundland

NEW FRANCE

Nova Scotia

Great Lakes

New England

LOUISIANA

ENGLISH COLONIES

Pennsylvania

Virginia

PACIFIC OCEAN

Carolina

TEXAS

Florida

ATLANTIC OCEAN

Gulf of Mexico

NEW SPAIN

SAINT DOMINGUE (Haiti)

CUBA

CARIBBEAN SEA

NEW GRANADA

English

French

Spanish

the New Netherland colonies, to an area at the mouth of the Delaware River.

Other ships had shorter journeys, and the emigrants were able to leave their ships much sooner. For example, within a week of sighting Mount Mansell, the emigrants on board the *Arabella* were preparing to disembark from the ship as it lay at anchor in Massachusetts Bay.

New Colonies, New Destinations, New Opportunities

As the European colonies in the New World grew in population and in number, later po-

tential colonists had the luxury to choose their destinations. New colonies that would become the modern states of South Carolina and Pennsylvania attracted specific groups of emigrants. William Penn, a practicing Quaker, advertised the forthcoming establishment of the new colony of Pennsylvania on the western shore of the Delaware River as a haven for Quakers and all other religions. His venture was a success, as Quakers and other dissenters voyaged from Europe directly to Pennsylvania. According to Alan Taylor, "during the early 1680s at least six hundred men subscribed for over 750,000 acres, raising about £9,000, which Penn needed to finance his new colony. About half of the investors eventually emigrated to Pennsylvania."[79]

Similar efforts by the organizers of what is now South Carolina were equally successful. They promised religious tolerance, but also appealed to wealthy investors in England and to established planters on the English island of Barbados, offering large land grants in the new colony. This encouraged several families to make a second New World voyage of sorts, as they left the New World islands of the Caribbean for the New World mainland. The decisions of the Middleton family of Barbados typify this period of many options. The father of the family planned to pass his entire large estate to the eldest of his three sons. The younger two left the island in 1667 and voyaged to the area around today's Charleston, South Carolina, to establish their own estates.

South Carolina and Pennsylvania became the destination of choice for many emigrants. But perhaps the most appealing option for potential emigrants in the last half of the 1600s who wished to pursue religious freedom was the colony of Rhode Island. From the earliest days of its founding, it became the colony of choice for religious dissenters from near and far.

"Rogue's Island"

The founders of what became the colony of Rhode Island had been religious dissenters

Roger Williams, founder of the Rhode Island colony, returns from England with the colony charter in 1644. The colony became a haven for religious dissenters.

themselves. Several of them had been banished from Massachusetts for being too radical for the Puritan leaders. As more and more religions dissenters ventured to the small colony surrounding Narragansett Bay, other colonial leaders labeled it "Rogue's Island" and branded it as a home of heretics and ruffians. Quakers who left Massachusetts, where they had been subject to public whippings and execution, were welcomed in Rhode Island. The first ship of Quaker colonists arrived in Rhode Island in 1657. Forty-five Huguenot families arrived from France in 1686, and headed to an area that is still known as Frenchtown, in the modern city of East Greenwich.

Jewish families arrived in Rhode Island from Europe to escape religious persecution. Some traveled directly from Spain and Portugal, but others arrived from colonies in the Caribbean and in South America. They had found that Spanish and Portuguese colonies in the New World continued the European practice of persecution, and relocated to Rhode Island to escape further discrimination. There were at least fifteen Jewish families in Newport by 1677, and other Jews made Rhode Island their destination of choice throughout the colonial period.

Finding Food and Shelter

Once the European emigrants arrived at their New World destination, their immediate attention was directed toward their basic needs of food and shelter. The supplies that they had purchased in Europe were offloaded from the ship, the animals that had survived the journey were penned in hastily built corrals, and the emigrants began to clear land to construct shelters and, if the season was right, to plant crops.

Although the passengers of the *Mayflower* had not arrived at their originally intended destination, they soon discovered distinct advantages to their landing site. Their disgruntlement at their immediate surroundings was soon tempered by an exploration of the nearby mainland, where they established a settlement they called Plymouth.

According to historian Taylor, they discovered villages and lands deserted by Native Americans whose relatives had been killed off by European diseases to which they had no immunity. Taylor writes that "the Plymouth colonists of New England in 1620 had their pick of recently abandoned Indian villages with conveniently clear land."[80] One colonist noted that these villages had once been home to thousands of Indians who had died in a recent plague, and remarked that "pity it was and is to see so many goodly fields, and so well seated, without men to dress and manure the same."[81]

These circumstances helped the early New England colonies to expand quickly, when other nations' colonists struggled to clear land and to coexist with the area's natives. Consequently, by 1630, English settlers had ranged along the coast of modern Massachusetts, and when the *Arabella* arrived, it was met by English families who were already in the area. Winthrop's diary records meeting many acquaintances already in the coastal settlements when they arrived, and being treated to a particularly fine dinner of venison and fresh beer.

African Arrivals in the New World

For thousands of new arrivals to the New World, there was little cause for celebration at reaching their ship's final destination, for

The Europeans Bring Disease

The arrival of Europeans to the New World brought more than new populations to the Western Hemisphere. One of the most devastating effects of the influx of Europeans was the introduction of European diseases to the Native American populations. After more than ten thousand years of isolation from contact with other continents, these people had no immunity to European afflictions.

Diseases such as smallpox, measles, bubonic plague, scarlet fever, diphtheria, pneumonia, whooping cough, and malaria came to the New World from Europe. Researcher Henry F. Dobyns, writing for the *Encyclopedia of North American Indians*, notes that the diseases took a devastating toll on the native population throughout the hemisphere.

"The second Columbian voyage to Hispaniola, in 1493, initiated the epidemic disease sequence. Most likely, domestic animals transported by Columbus's colonizing fleet harbored an influenza virus that spread among island natives, with catastrophic consequences. . . .

An English reconnaissance party on Roanoke Island in 1585 transmitted to its hosts an unidentified pathogen that killed scores of natives in each of the island's villages. . . .

By 1619, [bubonic plague] had spread northward [from Florida] to New England. So many Massachusetts [Indians] died that the Pilgrims, who arrived in 1620, persuaded themselves that God had destroyed the natives to open their territory to European colonists. . . .

In 1633, measles (or smallpox, or both) struck native peoples of New England. . . . In 1637, a different pathogen (most likely scarlet fever) swept through the same peoples. Two years later, smallpox spread through them. . . .

The diseases crossing the ocean during the sixteenth century usually caused so-called virgin-soil epidemics, because every Native American with whom they came in contact was susceptible. . . . Often entire families perished during virgin-soil epidemics because all members were stricken simultaneously, leaving no one capable of fetching water or preparing food."

they had not chosen to make the voyage. Those men, women, and children aboard slave vessels that completed the ocean crossing had little knowledge of what awaited them when they reached land, aside from what they had heard as rumors from fellow Africans before the voyage began. For the men, women, and children who reached the New World as human cargo in slave vessels, the sight of the New World was a time for despair.

African slaves arrived in the New World through many different ports. Portuguese slave ships arrived in the colony of Brazil; French slave ships arrived in the colony of Saint-Domingue off the island of Hispaniola; Dutch ships dropped anchor in the port of Curaçao in the Caribbean; Spanish ships ended their voyage at Cartagena in today's Colombia; and English slavers principally journeyed to Jamestown on the island of Barbados or Charleston in the colony of South Carolina. But no matter which port was the slave ship's ultimate destination, the experiences of the slaves during their arrival were quite similar.

The prisoners must have been puzzled when, upon reaching the port, the ship stayed offshore for several days—in some cases, even weeks—in quarantine before they were removed from their ship. According to Donald R. Wright,

Dangers of the voyage were not over with landfall. Africans who had become inured to a host of diseases endemic to their tropical homes were again in an environment with new diseases, new foods, and different water. Some ports required several weeks quarantine of arriving vessels, and it took days or weeks to arrange for sale.[82]

The port's officials were alerted to the ship's arrival and came to inspect the ship and

Jamestown colonists look on as the first African slaves arrive in the New World in 1619.

its cargo. The slaves were assembled on deck where they were listed and inspected, and a price tag was hung around each slave's neck. Sometimes prospective buyers came on board to inspect them as well.

Once the port officials deemed the ship's human cargo safe to be unloaded, the slaves were taken ashore and forced into shelters reminiscent of the African barracoons. One eyewitness to the barracoons of Cartagena called them "veritable cemeteries."[83]

However, the healthiest slaves were treated to a few days of decent food and allowed to rest, making them more presentable for sale; in some ports, they were given alcohol to make them less listless, and therefore more likely to sell. Those who were sold were put back into chains; in some Portuguese colonies they were branded once again, this time with the purchaser's name. Those who were not sold were usually less healthy; in some ports, they were released from their bonds. Without any food or aid from the local citizens, they wandered the waterfronts, ill and undernourished, until they died from starvation, exposure, or disease.

Adapting to a New Life

The thousands of Africans who arrived in the New World soon discovered that they would be torn from friends they had made on the slaving voyage and from any family members who were with them. European slave buyers were rarely concerned about such relation-

Jamestown settlers greet their wives as they come ashore. Husbands and sons typically established themselves in the colonies before family members joined them.

ships, often buying individuals without regard to family ties. The buyers were more interested in the slaves' physical condition than their personal histories.

Additionally, once the slaves had been transported to their new homes, they were burdened not only by their enforced servitude, but also by an inability to share their experiences with their fellow slaves. The other slaves could be from a dozen different African cultural groups; according to historian Hugh Thomas, one French colonial estate had "twenty-eight slaves from Allada [in modern Benin], three from the Gold Coast [near modern Ghana], six from the Calabar rivers [in modern Cameroon], eleven from near the river Congo, and nine from near the Senégal."[84] The newcomers had to learn to communicate with their fellow slaves, as well as learn the language of their new masters. Eventually they began to form new relationships and create new families, using the common language of their owners.

Friends and Family

For many of the European emigrants, knowing that family or friends awaited their arrival was a particularly strong motivation while aboard ship. Husbands and their sons often went ahead to begin their new life, and then sent back word on subsequent emigrant ships that the rest of the family should join them.

John Winthrop's wife, Margaret, and his six children arrived in Massachusetts in November 1631. But it must have been a bittersweet reunion for him. Margaret had been pregnant when Winthrop sailed from England, and she gave birth while he was still at sea aboard the *Arabella*. But the toddler died during her family's voyage, and was buried at sea. Winthrop never met her. Additionally, Margaret brought news that one of their sons had died suddenly before they left England.

In many ways, the experiences of John Winthrop typify the experiences of those who had voyaged to the New World. Winthrop's family experienced the joy of successfully crossing the Atlantic, the joy of reuniting with loved ones, and the pain of losing family members before and during the journey.

The Promise of the New World

The men, women, and children who crossed the Atlantic Ocean arrived in the New World with great hopes and dreams. Some, such as Roger Clap, found a new home in the first New World colony in which they arrived. Others, such as the Jews of Newport, Rhode Island, and the Middletons of South Carolina, moved from one colony to another in search of ideal conditions. And among the thousands of Africans enslaved in the New World, there were lingering memories of their homelands—and dreams of freedom.

These men, women, and children, from myriad religious, ethnic, and political backgrounds, struggled to bring their dreams of a new life in the New World to fruition. That was the promise of the New World. And for all who lived there, although their New World voyage had ended, their journey of life in the New World had only just begun.

Notes

Introduction:
A New World for Europeans

1. "Captain Arthur Barlowe's Narrative of the First Voyage to the Coasts of America," in ed. Henry S. Burrage, *Early English and French Voyages, Chiefly from Hakluyt, 1534–1608.* New York: Charles Scribner's Sons, 1906, p. 228.

Chapter 1: Ships and Crews

2. Quoted in Samuel Eliot Morison, *The Oxford History of the American People.* New York: Oxford University Press, 1965, pp. 28–29.
3. Samuel Eliot Morison, *The European Discovery of America: The Southern Voyages, 1492–1616.* New York: Oxford University Press, 1974, p. 54.
4. Samuel Eliot Morison, *The European Discovery of America: The Northern Voyages, A.D. 500–1600.* New York: Oxford University Press, 1971, p. 134.
5. David Beers Quinn, *Set Fair for Roanoke: Voyages and Colonies, 1584–1606.* Chapel Hill: University of North Carolina Press, 1985, p. 26.
6. Quoted in Morison, *European Discovery of America: The Northern Voyages,* p. 131.
7. Daniel Francis, "Transportation: 16th Century," *Pathfinders & Passageways: The Exploration of Canada,* National Library of Canada, December 7, 2001. www.collectionscanada.ca/explorers.
8. "Punishment of Seamen in the Reign of Queen Elizabeth," reproduced in *The Log Book; or, Nautical Miscellany.* London: Robins, 1830. www.corpun.com/kiss1.htm.

9. Quoted in Thomas Cavendish, *The Last Voyage of Thomas Cavendish, 1591–1592.* Chicago: University of Chicago Press, 1975, pp. 45–46.
10. Quoted in Cavendish, *Last Voyage,* p. 46.
11. Morison, *European Discovery of America: The Northern Voyages,* p. 190.

Chapter 2: Preparing to Emigrate

12. Quinn, *Set Fair for Roanoke,* p. 259.
13. Quoted in George Francis Dow, *Every Day Life in the Massachusetts Bay Colony.* Mineola, NY: Dover, 1988, pp. 10–11.
14. Marilyn C. Baseler, *"Asylum for Mankind": America, 1607–1800.* Ithaca, NY: Cornell University Press, 1998, p. 20.
15. Quoted in François Bellec, *Unknown Lands: The Log Books of the Great Explorers,* trans. Lisa Davidson and Elizabeth Ayre. Woodstock NY: Overlook Press, 2002, p. 109.
16. Bellec, *Unknown Lands,* p. 109.
17. Quinn, *Set Fair for Roanoke,* pp. 259–60.
18. "Letter from New England by Richard Saltonstall, 1631," *Proceedings of the Massachusetts Historical Society,* 2nd series, vol. iv, 1894. www.wadsworth.com/history_d/templates/student_resources/0030724791_ayers/sources/ch02/2.3.Saltonstall.html.
19. Roger Clap, *Memoirs of Capt. Roger Clap, Relating Some of God's Remarkable Providences to Him, in Bringing Him into New-England, and Some of the Straits and Afflictions, the Good People Met with Here, in There Beginnings. And Instructing, Counseling, Directing*

and *Commanding his Children, and Children's Children, and Household, to Serve the Lord in Their Generations to the Latest Posterity.* Boston: Greenleaf's Printing-Office, 1774, p. 6.

20. Quoted in Baseler, "*Asylum for Mankind,*" p. 35.

21. Baseler, "*Asylum for Mankind,*" p. 21.

22. Quoted in Baseler, "*Asylum for Mankind,*" pp. 50–51.

23. Quoted in Baseler, "*Asylum for Mankind,*" p. 50.

24. Quoted in Dow, *Every Day Life*, p. 3.

25. John Josselyn, *An Account of Two Voyages to New-England, Made During the Years 1638, 1663*, American Journeys: Eyewitness Accounts of Early American Exploration and Settlement: A Digital Library and Learning Center, 1865. www.americanjourneys.org/aj-107.

26. Quoted in Dow, *Every Day Life*, p. 7.

27. Mary N. Ganter, "Emigrants Crossing the Atlantic," *Early American Life*, February 1997, p. 44.

28. Ganter, "Emigrants," p. 44.

29. "Record of the Ship 'John Witherly,' 1635," in William Boys, *History of Sandwich*, 1786–1792; reprinted in the *New England Historical and Genealogical Register and Antiquarian Journal*, 1861. www.wadsworth.com/history_d/templates/student_resources/00307247 91_ayers/sources/ch02/2.1.migrants.html.

Chapter 3: Daily Life on a Voyage to the New World

30. Roger Daniels, *Coming to America: A History of Immigration and Ethnicity in American Life*, 2nd ed. New York: Perennial, 2002, pp. 49–50.

31. John Winthrop, entry for Wednesday, April 5, 1630, "The Voyage of the Fleet and Its Arrival in New England," *Shipboard Journal of John Winthrop*, The Winthrop Society, www.winthropsociety.org/journal.php.voyage.

32. Alan Taylor, *American Colonies.* New York, Viking, 2001, p. 168.

33. Charles Martyn, *The William Ward Genealogy: The History of the Descendants of William Ward of Sudbury, Mass., 1638–1925.* New York: Artemas Ward, 1925, p. 25.

34. Ganter, "Emigrants," p. 43.

35. Josselyn, *Account of Two Voyages*, p. 34.

36. Ganter, "Emigrants," p. 44.

37. Quoted in Dow, *Every Day Life*, p. 8.

38. Winthrop, entry for Thursday, May 20, 1630.

39. Winthrop, entry for Wednesday, April 14, 1630.

40. Daniels, *Coming to America*, p. 50.

41. Winthrop, entry for Thursday, May 27, 1630.

42. George Fox, *George Fox: An Autobiography*, ed. Rufus Jones, 1976, chap. 18. www.strecorsoc.org/gfox/ch18.html.

43. Anuradha Kumar, "Politics of Children's Games," *The Hindu*, March 24, 2002. www.hindu.com/thehindu/mag/2002/03/24.

Chapter 4: Hardship, Danger, and Death

44. Quoted in Taylor, *American Colonies*, p. 168.

45. Winthrop, entry for Monday, May 10, 1630.

46. Fox, *George Fox*, chap. 18.

47. Quoted in Dow, *Every Day Life*, p. 6.

48. D.P. Lyle, personal correspondence with the author, April 16, 2004.

49. Josselyn, *Account of Two Voyages*, p. 6.

50. Josselyn, *Account of Two Voyages*, p. 9.

51. Winthrop, entry for Tuesday, June 1, 1630.

52. Winthrop, entry for Tuesday, June 1, 1630.

53. D.P. Lyle, "What Was the State of Obstetric Medicine in 17th Century America?" The Writer's Medical and Forensics Lab, 2001. www.dplylemd.com/Questions/archive/obstetrics17thcentury.htm.

54. Winthrop, entry for Tuesday, April 6, 1630.

55. Fox, *George Fox*, Chap. 18.

56. Fox, *George Fox*, Chap. 18.

Chapter 5: Unwilling Emigrants

57. Quoted in Donald R. Wright, *African Americans in the Colonial Era: From African Origins Through the American Revolution*. Arlington Heights, IL: Harlan Davidson, 1990, p. 19.

58. Wright, *African Americans in the Colonial Era*, p. 25.

59. Quoted in Wright, *African Americans in the Colonial Era*, p. 32.

60. William D. Piersen, *From Africa to America: African American History from the Colonial Era to the Early Republic, 1526–1790*. New York: Twayne, 1996, p. 30.

61. Quoted in Wright, *African Americans in the Colonial Era*, p. 38.

62. Taylor, *American Colonies*, p. 326.

63. Piersen, *From Africa to America*, p. 24.

64. Piersen, *From Africa to America*, p. 32.

65. Wright, *African Americans in the Colonial Era*, p. 41.

66. Quoted in Hugh Thomas, *The Slave Trade: The Story of the Atlantic Slave Trade, 1440–1870*. New York: Simon & Schuster 1997, p. 420.

67. Quoted in Thomas, *Slave Trade*, p. 421.

68. Quoted in Thomas, *Slave Trade*, p. 428.

69. Quoted in Piersen, *From Africa to America*, p. 32.

70. Quoted in Thomas, *Slave Trade*, p. 412.

71. Phyllis Peres, "Forced Afro-Atlantic Migration and the Middle Passage," *Texts of Imagination and Empire: The Founding of Jamestown in its Atlantic Context*, The Folger Institute, Summer 2000. www.folger.edu/institute/jamestown/c_peres.htm.

Chapter 6: The Arrival

72. Diego Alvarez Chanca, "Letter of Dr. Chanca on the Second Voyage of Columbus," in Julius E. Olson and Edward G. Bourne, *The Northmen, Columbus and Cabot, 985–1503: The Voyages of the Northmen; The Voyages of Columbus and of John Cabot*. New York: Charles Scribner's Sons, 1906, p. 264.

73. Quoted in Taylor, *American Colonies*, p. 167.

74. Quoted in Taylor, *American Colonies*, p. 168.

75. William Bradford, *Bradford's History of Plimoth Plantation. From the Original Manuscript. With a Report of the Proceedings Incident to the Return of the Manuscript to Massachusetts. Printed Under the Direction of the Secretary of the Commonwealth, by Order of the General Court*. Boston: Wright & Potter Printing, State Printers, 1898, American Journeys: Eyewitness Accounts of Early American Exploration and Settlement: A Digital Library and Learning Center. www.americanjourneys.org/aj-025.

76. Alistair Cooke, *Alistair Cooke's America*. New York: Knopf, 1973, pp. 77–78.

77. Winthrop, entry for Tuesday, June 8, 1630.

78. Winthrop, entry for Tuesday, June 8, 1630.
79. Taylor, *American Colonies*, pp. 266–67.
80. Taylor, *American Colonies*, p. 44.
81. Quoted in Taylor, *American Colonies*, p. 44.
82. Wright, *African Americans in the Colonial Era*, p. 43.
83. Quoted in Taylor, *American Colonies*, p. 435.
84. Thomas, *Slave Trade*, p. 403.

For Further Reading

Books

François Bellec, *Unknown Lands: The Log Books of the Great Explorers*. Trans. Lisa Davidson and Elizabeth Ayre. Woodstock, NY: Overlook Press, 2002. Richly illustrated volume that covers the grand sweep of historical seaborne exploration, from the European discoveries of routes to the East Indies and the Americas to the explorations of the islands of the Pacific Ocean.

Thomas Cavendish, *The Last Voyage of Thomas Cavendish, 1591–1592*. Chicago: University of Chicago Press, 1975. A transcription of English explorer Thomas Cavendish's own report of his last voyage and his will; the transcription retains the sixteenth-century English spelling and usage, but remains a fascinating look into Cavendish's life and mind-set.

Alistair Cooke, *Alistair Cooke's America*. New York: Knopf, 1973. Personal essays interweaved with insightful history from one of the leading essayists of the last hundred years.

Tony Coulter, *Jacques Cartier, Samuel de Champlain, and the Explorers of Canada*. New York: Chelsea House, 1993. Part of the World Explorers series. Coulter examines France's sixteenth- and seventeenth-century efforts to establish a colony in Canada, focusing on the lives of the three explorers who first navigated the country's waterways.

Richard Hakluyt, *Hakluyt's Voyages to the New World: A Selection*. Indianapolis: Bobbs-Merrill, 1972. Hakluyt's original multivolume work from the sixteenth century is a classic collection of documents associated with the exploration and colonization of the New World by the English. This one-volume digest includes many of the highlights.

Jill Lepore, ed., *Encounters in the New World: A History in Documents*. New York: Oxford University Press, 2002. Part of the Pages from History series. From Columbus's voyage in 1492 to the publication of the autobiography of Olaudah Equiano, a former slave, in 1789, Lepore brings to life in exciting, first-person detail some of the earliest events in American history, seamlessly linking together primary sources that illustrate the powerful clash of cultures in the Americas.

Richard B. Morris and the Editors of *Life, The New World*. Vol. 1: *Prehistory to 1774*. New York: Time, 1963. Part of the *Life* History of the United States series. An accessible look at the formation of colonies and the interaction of the European and Indian empires.

Pablo E. Pérez-Mallaína, *Spain's Men of the Sea: Daily Life on the Indies Fleets in the Sixteenth Century*. Trans. Carla Rahn Phillips. Baltimore: Johns Hopkins University Press, 1998. The ships and men of Spain's Atlantic "treasure fleets," crucial to the country's empire in the New World during the sixteenth century, are discussed in lively detail from the sailors' backgrounds and motivations for going to sea to their life aboard the great galleons.

Janet Podell and Steven Anzovin, *Old Worlds to New: The Age of Exploration and Discovery*. New York: Wilson, 1993. Podell and Anzovin describe more than seventy-five interesting figures of the past six hundred years. Organized by area (empires of Portugal and Spain, North America, Africa, China and Japan) and such categories as "Science and Medicine" and "Mariners and Pirates," with chronological biographies in each section.

David Beers Quinn, *Set Fair for Roanoke: Voyagers and Colonies, 1584–1606*. Chapel Hill: University of North Carolina Press, 1985. The definitive examination of the Roanoke colonies. The twentieth-century archaeological evidence is now somewhat outdated by more recent excavations, but the historical background is unmatched.

Diane Sansevere-Dreher, *Explorers Who Got Lost*. New York: TOR, 1994. A richly illustrated treatment of early European explorers and their ships.

Loftin Snell, *The Wild Shores: America's Beginnings*. Washington, DC: National Geographic Society, 1974. Personal accounts of the author's search for the roots of the United States and Canada through visits to colonial and European sites.

Joseph Telushkin, *The Golden Land: The Story of Jewish Immigration to America: An Interactive History with Removable Documents and Artifacts*. New York: Harmony Books, 2002. Telushkin covers four centuries of Jewish immigration to the New World, from the first arrival of Jews to New Amsterdam in 1654 to the Lower East Side of New York City in the early twentieth century and other historical moments.

Web Sites

American Journeys (www.americanjourneys. org). This site of the Wisconsin Historical Society features a large collection of valuable narratives and descriptions of journeys to and throughout the Americas.

Celestial Navigation Net (www.celestial navigation.net). This site features a valuable collection of articles and images related to the essential art of celestial navigation—without which no explorer would have reached the New World.

The European Voyages of Exploration: The Fifteenth and Sixteenth Centuries (www.ucalgary.ca/applied_history/ tutor/eurvoya/index.htm). Emphasizing the rivalry between Spain and Portugal, this University of Calgary site examines the contributions of the two nations' mariners in global exploration.

The Mary Rose (www.maryrose.org). This fascinating Web site is dedicated to the sixteenth-century English warship the *Mary Rose*, which was constructed of an innovative design, and which sank, almost intact, in 1545. Today she is the subject of intense archaeological and historical research.

Pathfinders & Passageways: The Exploration of Canada (www.collectionscanada. ca/explorers/index-e.htm). This National Library of Canada site provides an excellent overview of some of the important European explorers of North America.

Works Consulted

Books

Charles M. Andrews, *The Colonial Period of American History*. Vol. 1: *The Settlements*. New Haven, CT: Yale University Press, 1934. A look at the development of the European colonies in the New World, with an emphasis on economic motivations.

Marilyn C. Baseler, *"Asylum for Mankind": America, 1607–1800*. Ithaca, NY: Cornell University Press, 1998. Excellent information about political and religious dissenters and their motivations to leave Europe.

Guy Meriwether Benson with William R. Irwin and Heather Moore Riser, *Lewis and Clark: The Maps of Exploration 1507–1814*. Charlottesville, VA: Howell Press, 2002. This book accompanied a special exhibition at the University of Virginia in conjunction with the upcoming Lewis and Clark bicentennial, but includes several maps from the early days of New World exploration.

Jeffrey P. Brain, Peter Copeland, Louis de la Haba, Mary Ann Harrell, Tee Loftin, Jay Luvaas, and Douglas W. Schwartz, *Clues to America's Past*. Washington, DC: National Geographic Society, 1976. A look at the archaeological legacy of both original inhabitants of and newcomers to the New World.

Francis J. Bremer, *John Winthrop: America's Forgotten Founding Father*. New York: Oxford University Press, 2003. An insightful study of Winthrop's life, religious beliefs, and governing style.

Henry S. Burrage, ed., *Early English and French Voyages, Chiefly from Hakluyt, 1534–1608*. New York: Charles Scribner's Sons, 1906. A collection of important narratives from the early days of European North American history, including the voyages of John White.

Roger Clap, *Memoirs of Capt. Roger Clap, Relating Some of God's Remarkable Providences to Him, in Bringing Him into New-England, and Some of the Straits and Afflictions, the Good People Met with Here, in There Beginnings. And Instructing, Counseling, Directing and Commanding his Children, and Children's Children, and Household, to Serve the Lord in Their Generations to the Latest Posterity*. Boston: Greenleaf's Printing-Office, 1774. A fascinating narrative about voyaging to, arriving in, and creating a new community in the New World.

Roger Daniels, *Coming to America: A History of Immigration and Ethnicity in American Life*. 2nd ed. New York: Perennial, 2002. A wide-ranging work about immigration; Part I ("Colonial America") concentrates on the pre-Revolution era.

George Francis Dow, *Every Day Life in the Massachusetts Bay Colony*. Mineola, NY: Dover, 1988. A comprehensive look at the lives, professions, architecture, and politics of the early days of modern Massachusetts. Chapter one examines the transatlantic voyages.

James Horn, *Adapting to a New World: English Society in the Seventeenth-Century Chesapeake*. Chapel Hill: University of North Carolina Press, 1994. Good information about emigrants' origins, social classes, and occupations.

John Camden Hotten, *The Original Lists of Persons of Quality; Emigrants; Religious Exiles; Political Rebels; Serving Men Sold for a Term of Years; Apprentices; Children Stolen; Maidens Pressed; and Others Who Went from Great Britain to the American Plantations, 1600–1700: With Their Ages, the Localities Where They Formerly Lived in the Mother Country, the Names of the Ships in Which They Embarked, and Other Interesting Particulars*. Salem, MA: Higginson, 1994. An excellent source for genealogical assistance. English ships' lists present a fascinating picture of seventeenth-century emigration.

Andrew Lambert, *War at Sea in the Age of Sail: 1650–1850*. London: Cassell, 2000. A richly illustrated book that examines naval warfare, tactics, ship design, and international politics.

Kris E. Lane, *Pillaging the Empire: Piracy in the Americas, 1500–1750*. Armonk, NY: M.E. Sharpe, 1998. A fascinating account of pirates and privateers, as well as the motivations of individuals and nations concerning such actions.

Charles Martyn, *The William Ward Genealogy: The History of the Descendants of William Ward of Sudbury, Mass., 1638–1925*. New York: Artemas Ward, 1925. Interesting narrative of the Ward family, including the arrival of William Ward in Massachusetts in 1638.

William McLoughlin, *Rhode Island: A Bicentennial History*. New York: W.W. Norton, 1978. An essential study of the development of the state over four centuries.

Milton Meltzer, ed., *In Their Own Words: A History of the American Negro, 1619–1865*. New York: Crowell, 1964. Interesting narratives, of which the first, Olaudah Equiano's "I Saw a Slave Ship", is the most germane to this project.

Samuel Eliot Morison, *The European Discovery of America: The Northern Voyages, A.D. 500–1600*. New York: Oxford University Press, 1971. The dean of American naval history recounts the first attempts at crossing the North Atlantic, along with European expeditions to today's Canada and New England.

———, *The European Discovery of America: The Southern Voyages, 1492–1616*. New York: Oxford University Press, 1974. Morison concentrates on the Spanish voyages and the first ones around the globe.

———, *The Oxford History of the American People*. New York: Oxford University Press, 1965. Morison provides both political and social history of the United States.

Julius E. Olson and Edward G. Bourne, eds., *The Northmen, Columbus and Cabot, 985–1503: The Voyages of the Northmen; The Voyages of Columbus and of John Cabot*. New York: Charles Scribner's Sons, 1906. A fascinating collection of letters and essays concerning the first voyagers to the New World.

Sir Charles Petrie, ed., *The Letters, Speeches and Proclamations of King Charles I*. London: Cassell, 1935. A collection of personal and royal writings from Charles I.

William D. Piersen, *From Africa to America: African American History from the Colonial Era to the Early Republic, 1526–1790*. New York: Twayne, 1996. Valuable insights into the origins and practices of the African slave trade.

Alan Taylor, *American Colonies*. New York: Viking, 2001. A wide-ranging examination of the exploration and exploitation of North America by Europeans during the fifteenth to eighteenth centuries.

Hugh Thomas, *The Slave Trade: The Story of the Atlantic Slave Trade, 1440–1870.* New York: Simon & Schuster, 1997. A fascinating look at the slave trade, with a large variety of first-person recollections.

Marianne Wokeck, *Trade in Strangers: The Beginnings of Mass Migration to North America.* University Park: Pennsylvania State University Press, 1999. Mostly concentrating on the late seventeenth and eighteenth centuries, this work includes information about Germans and Irish emigration, such as motivations and financing.

Donald R. Wright, *African Americans in the Colonial Era: From African Origins Through the American Revolution.* Arlington Heights, IL: Harlan Davidson, 1990. This volume covers the broad scope of the slave trade; excellent information about the myriad origins of the Africans, including their culture and beliefs.

Periodicals

Charles S. Brigham, ed., "British Royal Proclamations Relating to America, 1603–1783," *Transactions and Collections, American Antiquarian Society,* 1911.

Nancy D. Egloff, "'In the Service of Several Planters': Virginia's Early Africans," *Footsteps,* May/June 2002.

Mary N. Ganter, "Emigrants Crossing the Atlantic," *Early American Life,* February 1997.

Alison G. Olson, "Huguenots and Palatines," *Historian,* Winter 2001.

Jennifer Steinberg, "Last Voyage of the Slave Ship Henrietta Marie: A Grim Face on a European Jug, Relic from the Sunken Slave Ship Henrietta Marie, Witnessed the Horrors of Human Bondage. New Study of This Seventeenth-Century Vessel, the Oldest Slave Ship Ever Excavated, Helps Tell the Story of the Millions Whose Lives and Identities Were Lost." *National Geographic.* August 2002.

Internet Sources

William Bradford, *Bradford's History of Plimoth Plantation. From the Original Manuscript. With a Report of the Proceedings Incident to the Return of the Manuscript to Massachusetts. Printed Under the Direction of the Secretary of the Commonwealth, by Order of the General Court.* Boston: Wright & Potter Printing, State Printers, 1898; American Journeys: Eyewitness Accounts of Early American Exploration and Settlement: A Digital Library and Learning Center. www.americanjourneys.org/aj-025.

"Currency, Coinage & the Cost of Living: Pounds, Shillings & Pence: Purchasing Power 1674–1834," The Proceedings of the Old Bailey London, 1674–1834. www.oldbaileyonline.org/history/londonlife/coinage.html.

Roy Davies, "Current Value of Old Money," April 5, 2004. www.ex.ac.uk/~Davies/arian/current/howmuch.html.

John Davis, *The Seamans Secrets,* McAllen Memorial Library, 1594. www.mcallen.lib.tx.us/books/seasecr/dseasec1.htm.

Henry F. Dobyns, "Diseases," *Encyclopedia of North American Indians,* http://college.hmco.com/history/readerscomp/naind/html/na_010300_diseases.htm.

Kevin Archibald Forbes, "Admiral Sir George Somers Colonized Bermuda for Britain," Bermuda Online, February 17, 2004. www.bermuda-online.org/sirgeorgesomers.htm.

George Fox, *George Fox: An Autobiography.* Ed. Rufus Jones, 1976. www.strecorsoc.org/gfox/title.html.

Daniel Francis, "Transportation: 16th Century," *Pathfinders & Passageways: The Exploration of Canada*, National Library of Canada, December 7, 2001. www.collectionscanada.ca/explorers.

Garry Gillad and Reinhard Zierke, "Lowlands of Holland," Index of Martin Carthy's Songs and Times, March 5, 2003. www.informatik.uni-hamburg.de/~zierke/martin.carthy/songs/lowlandsofholland.html.

"The Impress Service," Broadside, October 6, 2003. www.nelsonsnavy.co.uk/broadside7.html.

Chris Jennings, "Where Did Shakespeare Set Prospero's Island in 'The Tempest'?" October 17, 2000. www.islomania.com/tempest/whereisprosperosisle.html.

John Josselyn, *An Account of Two Voyages to New-England Made During the Years 1638, 1663*, American Journeys: Eyewitness Accounts of Early American Exploration and Settlement: A Digital Library and Learning Center, 1865. www.americanjourneys.org/aj-107.

Anuradha Kumar, "Politics of Children's Games," *The Hindu*, March 24, 2002. www.hindu.com/thehindu/mag/2002/03/24.

"Letter from New England by Richard Saltonstall, 1631," *Proceedings of the Massachusetts Historical Society*, 2nd series, vol. iv, 1894. www.wadsworth.com/history_d/templates/student_resources/0030724791_ayers/sources/ch02/2.3.Saltonstall.html.

D.P. Lyle, "What was the State of Obstetrics in 17th Century America?" The Writer's Medical and Forensics Lab, 2001. www.dplylemd.com/Questions/archive/obstetrics17thcentury.htm.

Donald L. Miller, "The Plantation System and Indentured Servitude," *A Biography of America: English Settlement 1607–1691*, 2000. www.learner.org/biographyofamerica/prog02/transcript/page03.html.

"Navigational Instruments," Celestial Navigation Net, www.celestialnavigation.net/instruments.html.

"New Sweden or the Swedes on the Delaware," *Books, Maps and Prints Relating to New Sweden. Tercenteriary Commemorating the First Swedes and the Finns on the Delaware 1638–1938*, 1938. www.genealogia.fi/emi/art/article180e.htm.

Phyllis Peres, "Forced Afro-Atlantic Migration and the Middle Passage," *Texts of Imagination and Empire: The Founding of Jamestown in its Atlantic Context*, The Folger Institute, Summer 2000. www.folger.edu/institute/jamestown/c_peres.htm.

"Punishment of Seamen in the Reign of Queen Elizabeth," reproduced in *The Log Book; or, Nautical Miscellany* London: Robins, 1830. www.corpun.com/kiss1.htm.

"Record of Merchant Ship 'Hope,' July 1635," *New England Historical and Genealogical Register and Antiquarian Journal*, 1861. www.wadsworth.com/history_d/templates/student_resources.

"Record of the Ship 'John Witherly,' 1635," in William Boys, *History of Sandwich, 1786–1792*; reprinted in the *New England Historical and Genealogical Register and Antiquarian Journal*, 1861. www.wadsworth.com/history_d/templates/student_resources/0030724791_ayers/sources/ch02/2.1.migrants.html.

"Record of Ship 'The Confidence,' April 1638," Olive Tree Genealogy, http://olivetreegenealogy.com.

"A Slave Ship Speaks: The Wreck of the *Henrietta Marie*," Mel Fisher Maritime Heritage Society, 2001. www.melfisher.org/henriettamarie/middlepassage.htm.

"Smallpox," Dittrick Medical History Center, Case Western Reserve University, 2003. www.cwru.edu/artsci/dittrick/smallpox/disease-description.htm.

"The Terrible Transformation," *Africans in America*, WGBH-TV, 1998. www.pbs.org/wgbh/aia/part1/title.html.

Edward Waterhouse, "Necessary Supplies for the Voyage to Virginia, 1622," *A Declaration of the State of the Colony and Affairs in Virginia*, 1622. www.wadsworth.com/history_d/templates/student_resources/0030724791_ayers/sources/ch02/2.1.waterhouse.htm.

Marilyn J. Westerkamp, "Indentured Servitude," *Reader's Companion to U.S. Women's History*, http://college.hmco.com/history/readerscomp/women/html/wm_017400_indenturedse.htm.

Samuel Williamson, "Comparing the Purchasing Power of Money in Great Britain from 1264 to 2002," How Much Is That? EH.net. http://eh.net/hmit/ppowerbp.

John Winthrop. "The Voyage of the Fleet and Its Arrival in New England," *Shipboard Journal of John Winthrop*, The Winthrop Society, www.winthropsociety.org/journal.php-voyage.

Index

Picture Credits

Cover: © Nasjonalgalleriet, Oslo, Norway/
  Bridgeman Art Library
© Bettmann/CORBIS, 28, 35, 37, 47, 49, 53,
  57, 66, 70, 92
© CORBIS, 11, 33, 85, 91
Corel Corporation, 50
© Tria Giovan/CORBIS, 22
©Hulton Archive/Getty Images, 32, 39, 41,
  63, 72, 76, 78, 79

© James Marshall/CORBIS, 58
National Library of Medicine/Photo Re-
  searchers, Inc., 61
Brandy Noon, 15, 20, 45, 54, 87
North Wind Picture Archives, 74, 83, 88
Bildarchiv Preussicher Kulturbesitz/Art Re-
  source, NY, 19
Joseph Paris Picture Archive, 17, 21, 27
Photos.com, 10, 13, 25

About the Author

Andrew A. Kling is a native of Providence, Rhode Island, and has been fascinated with history for as long as he can remember. A career with the National Park Service included three years at Fort Raleigh National Historic Site, which commemorates the first English attempts at settlement in the New World.

He currently lives in Montana, where he works as a freelance writer, editor, interpretive media developer, and consultant.